FINLAND

RUSSIA

BALTIC SEA

POLAND

「Escape」

⌈Escape⌋

*A Jewish Scandinavian family
in the Second World War*

NORMAN S. POSER

SAREVE PRESS ~ NEW YORK

International Standard Book Number 0-9785910-0-3

Designed and edited by Carol Haralson, Sedona, Arizona

*Photograph, page 2: Members of the Salomon family in Voksenlia, Norway,
summer of 1932. Left to right around the table: Else, Max, Norman, Gerda,
Johanna, Grete. Foreground: Joe.*

SAREVE PRESS

290 West End Avenue (Suite 10D)

New York, New York 10023

Printed in Canada

for Grete, my mother

CONTENTS

AFTERMATH

MAPS

NORWEGIAN SEA
SWE
NORWAY
Oslo
NORTH SEA
UNITED
KINGDOM
DENMARK
Copenhage
GERMANY
Berlir

The Salomon Family

Salomon
1853–1893

m.

Marta Clara Kelm
1853–?

Leopold
1856–?

Anny
1900–1916

Hans
1902–1962

m.

Gunvor Petersen
b. 1914

Willy Jarl
1903–?

Marcus Victo
1905–2001

CHILDREN OF MAX AND NORA

Frøydis, b. 1938
Birgit, b. 1941
Robert, b. 1943

CHILD OF GERDA

Dorrit
1934–2001

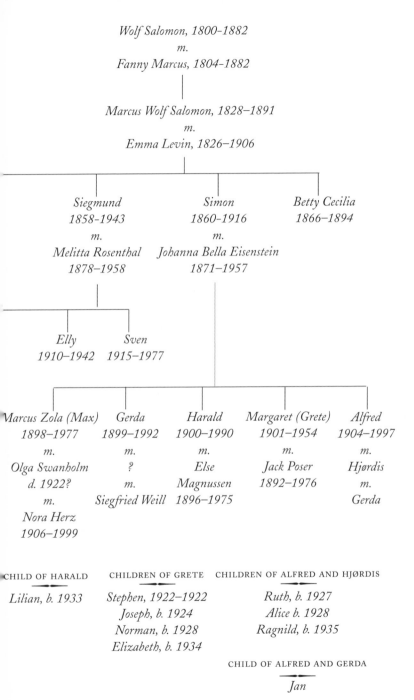

Wolf Salomon, 1800–1882
m.
Fanny Marcus, 1804–1882

Marcus Wolf Salomon, 1828–1891
m.
Emma Levin, 1826–1906

Siegmund	Simon	Betty Cecilia
1858-1943	1860-1916	1866–1894
m.	m.	
Melitta Rosenthal	Johanna Bella Eisenstein	
1878-1958	1871–1957	

| Elly | Sven |
| 1910–1942 | 1915–1977 |

Marcus Zola (Max)	Gerda	Harald	Margaret (Grete)	Alfred
1898–1977	1899–1992	1900–1990	1901–1954	1904–1997
m.	m.	m.	m.	m.
Olga Swanholm	?	Else	Jack Poser	Hjørdis
d. 1922?	m.	Magnussen	1892–1976	m.
m.	Siegfried Weill	1896–1975		Gerda
Nora Herz				
1906–1999				

CHILD OF HARALD CHILDREN OF GRETE CHILDREN OF ALFRED AND HJØRDIS

Lilian, b. 1933 Stephen, 1922–1922   Ruth, b. 1927
      Joseph, b. 1924   Alice b. 1928
      Norman, b. 1928   Ragnild, b. 1935
      Elizabeth, b. 1934

CHILD OF ALFRED AND GERDA

Jan

RESEARCHING AND WRITING this book have been an extraordinary adventure. It has taken my wife, Judy, and me to Denmark, Norway, Sweden, and the German province of Schleswig-Holstein. Along the way, we met many generous, knowledgeable, and hospitable people, including Danish and Norwegian relatives, without whose help the book could not have been written. I learned more about the history of my family than I had ever dreamed possible. Also, writing about my mother's sudden, dreadful death more than fifty years ago and about my parents' relationship with each other has helped liberate me from the past.

The main purpose of writing the book is to hand on to my children, grandchildren, nephews, nieces, and cousins a permanent record of the saga of the Salomon family. I believe, however, that it will be of interest to a broader audience because it enlarges our knowledge of the response of the Scandinavian countries (other than Finland) to the Holocaust. With the exception of the well known story of the Danish rescue of that country's Jewish population in October 1943, what happened in Scandinavia during the war is not well known to the world. Some of the events described here, such as the successful efforts of the Danish consul in Oslo in the winter of 1942-43 to save many of the Danish Jews living in Norway, have never (to my knowledge) been published before.

This is a factual account, based largely on contemporaneous sources. Where I have drawn conclusions from conflicting or insufficient data, I so indicate. I was fortunate to have access to an extensive correspondence written by my grandmother and other family members from Scandinavia during and shortly after the war. These letters, many of which were written in occupied Norway as events were unfolding, provide a vivid and invaluable historical record of events. The book is also based on personal recollections, interviews with family members, and records in Danish and Norwegian government archives. To place the events in their historical context, I have used published literature about the German occupation of Norway and Denmark; the fate of their Jewish populations; and the role that Sweden played, not always enthusiastically, as a haven for Jewish refugees from the Nazis.

I am indebted to a long list of people, some of them no longer living.

It was my aunt, Gerda Weill, who launched me on this project in 1970 when she told me what she knew about the origins of my mother's family, the Salomons in Schleswig-Holstein and about her (and my mother's) childhood in Norway during the early years of the twentieth century.

On my two visits to Denmark and Norway in 1948 and 1977, my uncles Max and Harald told me something (but actually very little) about their wartime experiences. If only I had had more curiosity at the time and asked them more questions. On my second visit, Harald pointed out to me and my daughter the house in central Copenhagen where his father (my grandfather) was born in 1860, not long after his father immigrated to Denmark.

Two historians, Bjarte Bruland in Norway and Vilhjal-mur Orn Vilhjalmsson in Denmark, gave me valuable information about Scandinavia during the war and identified for me relevant government archives. Leif Thingrud, archivist, and Ellen Risj, head of section, of the Oslo City Archives were extremely cooperative and helpful in giving me access to information about the early history of my family in Norway. Victor Lind provided me with information about the Holocaust in Norway.

I am greatly indebted to the historian Professor William Hitchcock of Temple University for his tremendously helpful and incisive comments on a draft of the manuscript of this book.

Elsebeth Paikin is probably the foremost living expert on Jewish Scandinavian genealogy. She took Judy and me to two Jewish cemeteries in Copenhagen, the Mosaic Northern Cemetery in Mollegade, which contains graves dating back to the seventeenth century, and the Western Cemetery, where my grandparents, Simon and Johanna Salomon, are buried. As a result of Ms. Paikin's search of the archives, I learned who my Danish great-grandparents were. Leif Rosenstock, who as a child was one of the Danish Jews rescued in October 1943, gave freely of his time to research nineteenth century Copenhagen archives on my behalf and unearthed valuable information about my Danish ancestors. Sad to say, Mr. Rosenstock died in 2004.

Leo Goldberger, who as a boy also was rescued from Denmark in October 1943 and has written perceptively about the Danish rescue, gave me useful guidance on people to see and places to go in Denmark. My friend, Ernest Nives, a survivor of Auschwitz and an assiduous chronicler of the Holocaust, continually encouraged me to do the research for this book and also put me in touch with several people in Europe who could be of assistance. My friend and law school classmate Michael Finkelstein gave me useful advice on how to approach the writing of the book.

The United States Holocaust Museum and its library staff provided materials on the Swedish response to the Holocaust. The American-Scandinavian Foundation in New York sponsored two excellent lecture programs during 2003 — one on the rescue of the Danish Jews and the other on Jewish life and culture in Norway — which gave me information and fresh insights into the response of these two countries to the Holocaust.

One of the unexpected pleasures of undertaking this project was meeting two people who generously gave their time to help me with the research.

The first is Ole Harck, professor of archeology at Christian-Albrechts-Universitaet in Kiel. He gave me the benefit of his encyclopedic knowledge and understanding of Jewish history in Schleswig-Holstein. Professor Harck's exhaustive study of the inscriptions on the tombstones in the Jewish cemetery in Kiel provided additional information about my ancestors.

The second is Ragnar Areklett, a retired Norwegian schoolteacher who has devoted his retirement years to studying and writing about the Holocaust in Norway. He voluntarily undertook to do research about the Salomon family and the Salomon Shoe Factory. He also arranged a visit for us to the Bredtvedt prison in Oslo where my grandmother was held for three anxious, if not terrifying, months in 1942-43.

I owe an enormous debt to my Scandinavian researchers. Ingvil Eilertsen Grimstad was relentless and resourceful in tracking down information about the family in archives in Oslo as well as in Stockholm and Gothenburg. After Ms. Grimstad completed her studies at Oslo University, Marta Gjernes continued her excellent work. In Copenhagen, Malthe Sørensen found a large amount of immensely valuable material for me in the Danish State Archives, particularly on the circumstances of my grandmother's release from prison in Norway and her return to Denmark in 1943.

Solveig Kjøk, a Norwegian visual artist and professional translator who lives in Brooklyn, New York, translated into beautiful English a large number of letters, archival materials, and articles from Norwegian and some from Danish and German. Her language skills and sensitivity are apparent throughout the book, for I have quoted copiously from her translations. Ms. Kjøk also helped me find my excellent Norwegian and Danish researchers.

I am immensely grateful to Carol Haralson, who edited the manuscript and designed the book with highly professional skill, artistry, and enthusiasm.

Several relatives gave me vital information for the book. My cousin Lilian Birdi, Harald Salomon's daughter, told Judy and me about her escape from Denmark with her parents in October 1943. Lilian and her husband Kulbir took us to the fisherman's shack where the family hid at night waiting for the fishing boat that would take them to Sweden. Lilian also generously gave me written materials about her father and his career.

My cousins Frøydis Moe Petersen and Robert Salomon,

Max Salomon's children, helped me greatly to understand the lives of my grandparents and their father. Through Frøydis and Robert, we met Elizabeth Skjelsvik, who had known my grandmother during the 1940s, and who was kind enough to give me a batch of letters that my grandmother wrote to her from Denmark and Sweden during and after the war years.

Another cousin Dorrit Berg, Gerda Weill's daughter, described for me in great detail her escape with her mother from Norway in 1940 and their six-month journey through Sweden, the Soviet Union, Japan, and Canada, to the United States. Dorrit also gave me information about my mother's early years. Sadly, Dorrit died in 2001. Dorrit's three children, Kevin, Eric, and Sonia Berg, Kevin's wife Noreen, and Dorrit's long-time partner, Nancy Stanich, made available to me a treasure trove of letters, written from Scandinavia during the war, and photographs that Gerda had kept in cardboard boxes and had passed on to Dorrit, who left them untouched in her garage.

My second cousin, Leif Salomon (the grandson of my grandfather's brother Siegmund) told me the story of his parents' unsuccessful attempt to escape from Norway to Sweden and the birth of his older sister, Hanne, in the Norwegian forest in June 1940. Fortunately, the family, including Leif, who was born in 1941, eventually succeeded in leaving Norway; that is one of the stories told in this book. Hanna and Leif's mother Gunvor, now over ninety and living in Denmark, was kind enough to provide many details of their wartime experience, even though she was understandably reluctant to relive these horrible events.

I thank my brother, Joseph Poser, and my sister, Liz Gribin, for sharing with me their recollections of events relating to my family. I am particularly grateful to Liz for agreeing to revisit the painful memory of the circumstances surrounding our mother's death in 1954. I also thank my son, Sam, for the interest and encouragement he gave me throughout the five years of this book's gestation.

Above all, I want to thank my daughter, Susan, and my wife, Judy. From the beginning, Susan maintained a continuous and active interest in the researching and writing this book. She read drafts and gave me enormously helpful and perceptive suggestions. She encouraged me to keep working on it when other commitments tempted me to put it aside. Judy read source material and drafts and gave me valuable comments on the organization and structure of the book. She also was my companion on two visits to Scandinavia (in 2001 and 2004) where she helped me enormously with the research. Our discussions of the book as its progressed were wonderfully productive. Words cannot adequately express how much I appreciate her patience and her devotion to the project.

NORMAN S. POSER

APRIL 2006

NEW YORK CITY

INTRODUCTION

———◆———

APRIL 9, 1940

WHEN MAX SALOMON looked out the window of his home on Oslo Fjord the morning of April 9, 1940, he could see warplanes landing at Fornebu Airport. German troops were flooding into Norway and meeting almost no resistance. Max and his wife Nora quickly packed their small car with diapers and other paraphernalia they would need for their infant daughter Frøydis and, with Frøydis in Nora's arms, drove toward the Swedish border. Max, a forty-two-year-old businessman, had a special reason to flee the country of his birth. He was a member of Norway's small Jewish population.

Max's sister Gerda Weill also was in Norway when the Germans invaded. Forty-one and twice divorced, she lived with her only child, five-year-old Dorrit, and her widowed mother. Gerda had lived in Berlin in the early days of the Hitler regime and had no illusions about German intentions toward the Jews. She withdrew her money from an Oslo bank and headed for the railroad station with Dorrit, hoping to board the next train to Sweden.

Johanna, Max and Gerda's mother, had been born in Poland and brought up in Germany, but she had married a Danish Jew and moved to Norway in the 1890s. She was widowed in 1916. In 1940, she was settled in her ways and accustomed to dominating her five children. She rejected her daughter's urgent advice to leave the country. A friend named Sverre Helliksen (who was arrested after the war as a Nazi collaborator) persuaded Johanna that the Germans would do her no harm. Why would the Germans want to harm an old woman? Like most Norwegian Jews in 1940, she decided to stay. Johanna would be imprisoned in a Norwegian concentration camp when the Norwegian police rounded up the Norwegian Jews in late 1942, but, with the help of the Danish consul-general in Oslo, would narrowly escape deportation to Auschwitz.

Two of Johanna's five children lived in Denmark, which also fell to the German invasion that morning without a struggle. Harald, Johanna's third child, was without doubt the most successful member of the family. Born in Norway in 1900, he had become a Danish citizen in 1927. He was a highly talented and well known sculptor, who held the post of medalist of the Royal Danish Mint. For thirty years — before, during, and after the war — he designed Denmark's coins and the commemorative medals struck for special occasions, such as royal birthdays and marriages. He and his wife Else, who was not Jewish, lived in modest comfort in Copenhagen with their seven-year-old daughter, Lilian. Because German occupation authorities allowed the Danish government to manage its own internal affairs until the summer of 1943, the occupation did not at first affect Harald in any important way. Nonetheless, he felt what he later described as the occupation's "hard knife edge of terror" along with Denmark's other 8,000 Jews. In October 1943, Harald and his family escaped to Sweden when the Danish people, in a unique and heroic episode of the Holocaust, defied their German masters to save nearly all the Danish Jews.

The youngest of Johanna's children was Alfred, aged thirty-six. He was married and had three young daughters. Alfred's life had been turbulent and unhappy. In 1940, his marriage was breaking up, and he was suffering from a serious mental illness that was greatly exacerbated by a totally rational fear of the Germans. Alfred remained in Denmark throughout the war, much of the time hidden from the Germans in a mental institution.

The only one of Johanna's five children who was not in Norway or Denmark at the time of the invasion was Margaret, always known in the family as Grete (or Grethe). She had married Jack Poser, a Jewish fur dealer from Cracow, in 1921 and settled in England. In 1939, shortly after the war began, she moved to New York with her husband and their three children, Joseph, Elizabeth, and myself. On April 10, 1940, when news of the German invasion of Denmark and Norway was headlined in the New York newspapers, Grete spent the morning weeping hysterically in bed.

As it turned out, Johanna, Max, Gerda, Harald, and Alfred all survived the Holocaust. Their story is on the whole a happy as well as an unusual one. The war years were difficult for Max but, paradoxically, perhaps the most personally fulfilling of his life. Gerda suffered economic hardship after fleeing Norway for the United States, but she discovered new strengths and resources in herself. Harald's escape from Denmark in October 1943 and his exile in Sweden for nineteen months resulted in new professional achievements as well as pride in the role he played in the Danish Brigade, which helped liberate Copenhagen from the Germans. In entirely different ways and under different circumstances, all three proved themselves equal to daunting challenges. Alfred remained fragile but was sheltered from deportation in a Danish mental institution. Ironically, Grete, who had the good fortune to be living in affluence in New York during the war years, met a tragedy the others escaped.

There is only one exception to the Salomons' escape from the Holocaust: Elly Salomon, Johanna's niece. Elly's father, Siegmund Salomon, and Johanna's husband, Simon Salomon, were brothers. When the Germans invaded Norway, Elly was thirty and unmarried, living alone in Oslo. During the early morning hours of November 26, 1942, she was arrested by the Norwegian police, taken directly in a commandeered taxi to a prison ship waiting in Oslo harbor, turned over there with over 500 other Norwegian Jews to the German SS, and murdered in a gas chamber within hours after her arrival at Auschwitz.

Whether a Jew lived or died during the German occupation of Norway was at least partly a matter of luck. Elly Salomon was one of the unlucky ones. Her brother Hans tried to leave Norway with his family in 1940, but was turned back at the border by Swedish officers. Unlike his sister, Hans survived; he was imprisoned in a Norwegian concentration camp in late 1942, but permitted to leave the following year with his Swedish, non-Jewish wife and two children after establishing that he was a Danish citizen. Johanna too survived because she was lucky; by happenstance, she wasn't living at home when the Norwegian police came around to arrest all Jewish women and children. She was imprisoned in Oslo two weeks later, but by that time the doomed Norwegian Jews, including her niece Elly, had been taken by ship to Stettin in Germany and from there to Auschwitz. The two-week delay allowed the Danish consul-general in Oslo to obtain her release from prison and her repatriation to Denmark on the basis of Danish citizenship. Seven months later, Johanna was again forced to escape from the Nazis, this time to Sweden.

None of Johanna's children thought of themselves primarily as Jewish or was an active member of a Jewish congregation. Although Johanna was the daughter of a rabbi, she had lived in Scandinavia most of her life, and when the Germans invaded Norway she apparently believed herself no different from other Norwegians. But virulent anti-Semitism (both Norwegian and German) found the Salomons nonetheless. Even Harald was forced to flee tolerant, democratic Denmark because of his Jewish birth. The Salomons may have lacked a strong feeling of Jewish identity, but their experience during the war was perforce that of a Jewish family.

⌈Origins⌋

Gråbrødre Torv, the square in Copenhagen where the Salomons were living in 1860 when Simon Salomon was born. (Courtesy of Copenhagen Bymuseum)

SWEDEN

Gothenburg

KATTEGAT

DENMARK

Hornbaek

Copenhagen

Leck

SCHLESWIG-HOLSTEIN

(GERMANY
AFTER 1864)

Kiel

Altona

Schleswig-Holstein
and Denmark

{1828-1893}

FAMILY LEGEND has it that for at least a century the Salomon family lived in Schleswig-Holstein, the two duchies on the rainy, foggy plain that lies at the base of the Jutland peninsula, astride the border between Denmark and Germany.[1] With the exception of the Danish-speaking part of Schleswig (the northernmost of the two duchies), Schleswig-Holstein was almost entirely German-speaking; but from medieval times until 1864, both duchies were ruled by the Danish king.[2] The duchies were not an integral part of Denmark but were administered through a separate government body in Copenhagen, the so-called "German Chancellory." They had their own laws, including special laws that applied to their Jewish populations.

Jews had made Schleswig-Holstein their home since at least the seventeenth century. They lived restricted lives, separate and apart from the rest of the population. Local authorities required them to be members of the local synagogue, which was responsible not only for religious functions but also for many other facets of community life, such as care of the poor and sick, and education of the young. The separate Jewish and Christian communities generally lived in peace with each other, but some Schleswig-

Holstein cities and towns strictly limited the number of Jews permitted to reside there and prohibited them from exercising most professions and occupations. The principal Holstein city was Kiel, situated on a magnificent harbor in the Baltic Sea on the eastern coast of Jutland. In 1844, Kiel had only sixty-two Jews, most of them making a living dealing in textiles, clothing, and second-hand goods. A Jewish physician (presumably not a resident of Kiel) observed in 1849: "Beside the small trade, I don't know of any other livelihood permitted to the local Jews; even those who have learned a craft have returned to [selling] junk."[3]

Marcus Salomon, the patriarch of the Scandinavian Salomons, was born on April 1, 1828, in Altona, a city in Holstein on the north bank of the Elbe River just west of the great German port of Hamburg.[4] It is likely that Marcus went to school in Altona, but he lived and worked in Kiel as a young man. It is tempting to speculate that Marcus's connection with Altona had a significant influence on his life and that of his descendants. Although deep within the German-speaking duchy of Holstein, Altona had been under Danish rule since 1640 and had close ties with Denmark.[5] The local authorities were more tolerant toward Jews than were the governing bodies of other Schleswig-Holstein towns. The Jewish elementary school in Altona, unlike other Jewish schools in the two duchies, used the Danish language in the classroom rather than German. Marcus Salomon's decision as a young man to move to Denmark may have been partly due to pro-Danish sentiments that he had acquired as a schoolboy.

Marcus's wife also was a member of the Jewish community of Schleswig-Holstein. Emma Levin (or Lewin) was born on September 8, 1826,[6] in the small

German-speaking village of Leck on the west coast of Schleswig, near Fredrikstad, just south of the present German-Danish border. Fredrikstad, like other Schleswig-Holstein towns, had a ghetto-like Jewish community. It was the only town in Schleswig with a synagogue and a Jewish cemetery. As a young couple, Marcus and Emma lived in Kiel, where Marcus engaged in commerce, probably selling shoes and other articles of clothing.

Because Schleswig-Holstein was ruled by Denmark but was mostly German in its language and sentiments, it existed in a chronic state of military and diplomatic crisis. In the mid-nineteenth century, the relations between Denmark and the two duchies were both bitter and extraordinarily complex. Lord Palmerston, the British prime minister, famously said that only three persons in the world understood the Schleswig-Holstein question: the first was Queen Victoria's consort Prince Albert, who unfortunately was dead; the second was a Danish statesman, who had become insane; and the third was Palmerston himself, who had forgotten what he knew about it.[7] The dispute between Denmark and the German states over Schleswig-Holstein led to two wars, the first in 1848-51 and the second in 1864.

The underlying cause of these wars was an upsurge of nationalistic feeling, a phenomenon that manifested itself in revolutions throughout continental Europe in 1848. The German majority in Schleswig-Holstein was determined to throw off Danish rule, and their aspirations were backed by Prussia and Austria, the two most powerful German states. The situation of the Schleswig-Holsteiners — and their capacity to make trouble — was similar to that of the Sudeten Germans of Czechoslovakia in the 1930s.[8]

Seventy years before Hitler's rise to power, an English journalist observed presciently of the Schleswig-Holsteiners: "It is strange to see how bitter, how violent, these Germans can be when they have managed to lash themselves into a passion."[9] The Danes, for their part, also were fiercely nationalistic; many of them wished to create a greater Denmark that would incorporate within its borders all of Schleswig (the northern duchy), both its German-speaking and its Danish-speaking population. Given the dominant position of Germany in Europe, this was an unrealistic goal, and its pursuit brought great harm to Denmark.

In March 1848, the Danish government proposed to adopt a new constitution which would link Schleswig more closely with Denmark.[10] Viewing this action as a provocation which promised to separate the two duchies and make Schleswig an integral part of Denmark, the Schleswig-Holsteiners rebelled.[11] The rebels, supported by 12,000 Prussian soldiers, drove deep into Denmark; but they were beaten back and eventually defeated by an outnumbered Danish army.[12]

Despite their defeat, the Schleswig-Holstein nationalists continued to agitate for independence from Denmark. They established their headquarters in Kiel, which a correspondent for the *London Times* in 1864 described as "a slippery town, slovenly, narrow streets, mean houses, meaner shops."[13] There is nothing left today of nineteenth-century Kiel because, as the principal German naval base during World War II, it was leveled by Allied bombers and was rebuilt after the war as a modern but rather characterless city. In 1864, the Schleswig-Holsteiners attacked Denmark again and, with the help of German military power, succeeded in throwing off Danish rule. Prussia annexed all of

Schleswig-Holstein, not only German-speaking Holstein and southern Schleswig but also northern Schleswig, which was (and still is) largely Danish-speaking. After Germany's defeat in the First World War, the Danish-speaking northern part of Schleswig was restored to Denmark. The remainder of Schleswig-Holstein is now a province of Germany.

The mid-nineteenth century was not a peaceful or reassuring time for a Jewish merchant in Kiel. The provisional government of Schleswig-Holstein in Kiel had emancipated the Jews in 1848, probably in order to gain their support in the Schleswig-Holsteiners' attempt that year to break free from Danish rule.[15] After Denmark defeated the Schleswig–Holsteiners in the first Dano-German war, the two duchies revoked the laws emancipating the Jews. In 1853, the Kiel municipal authorities, acting at the behest of the guild of shopkeepers, who feared commercial competition, attempted to expel the Jews from the city. The Jewish residents turned for help to the Danish king, who refused to overrule the Kiel city fathers but said that he would consider each case individually. This left the affected families uncertain as to their future. It is possible that Marcus Salomon and his family decided to leave Kiel rather than wait to see how their case would be decided. In 1858 (not long after Marcus had emigrated to Denmark), the shopkeepers' guild, writing in a "tone of hostility and personal spite," again protested against the permanent residence of Jews in the city.[16] The Jewish population of Holstein had to wait until 1863 to receive the civil rights the Danish Jews had enjoyed since 1849.

It is likely that Marcus Salomon not only chafed under anti-Semitic restrictions imposed on him in Kiel, but also saw attractive business opportunities in Denmark and the other countries of Scandinavia. At least a decade before his move to Copenhagen, he had established business connections there. As a very young man, he visited the city on business in 1845 and again in 1847. That he was well-to-do is indicated by the fact that on both visits to Copenhagen he stayed at Hotel Angleterre, then (as now) the city's most luxurious hotel. His parents, Wolf and Fanny (Marcus) Salomon, who both died in 1882 and are buried in the Kiel cemetery, appear to have been relatively prosperous.

Marcus and Emma Salomon settled in Copenhagen sometime between 1853 and 1856. Life for a Jew was much freer there than in Kiel. Denmark had a long history of toleration for minorities. Sephardic Jews had been allowed to live in the country since 1622, when King Christian IV invited Jews from Amsterdam and Hamburg to settle in the newly established town of Glückstadt on the River Elbe. In 1809, Denmark gave Jews the right to live wherever they wanted in Denmark. In 1814, a royal decree of King Frederick VI permitted Jews to engage in any trade or profession, although they still could not vote. In return for their newly won rights, Jews were required to obey the laws of Denmark, rather than the rabbinical regulations and customs under which they had previously lived.[17]

Danish Jews finally received full political equality under the constitution of 1849, which totally integrated the country's Jews into the general population. The constitution stated: "No one shall be prevented from exercising his full civil and political rights by virtue of his religious faith, but no one shall be permitted to evade his general civic duties by virtue of this faith."[18]

Copenhagen in the 1850s was a far cry from the clean, sophisticated city that residents and visitors alike enjoy today. The botanist J.W. Hornemann wrote at the time: "Copenhagen is a very filthy city. Everyone who enters the city gates from the countryside is immediately struck by the bad air."[19] The city was overcrowded, suffused with a persistent stench from the tanneries, rotting meat, stagnant gutters, fish blood, swamps, match factories, and latrine dumps, among other things. Excrement — called "night soil" — was collected in cellars, which were emptied only once or twice a year. Not surprisingly, it came into contact with the city's drinking water, and as a result there were sporadic outbreaks of cholera, one of them occurring in 1853, not long before Marcus Salomon and his family moved to Copenhagen.[20]

Marcus and Emma had four sons and a daughter, all of whom survived into adulthood. Our concern in this narrative is with two of their sons, Simon and Siegmund, who later emigrated to Norway. At first, the Salomons lived on Holmensgade, a street near the harbor in an area that had a rather shady reputation as a hangout for sailors and prostitutes. Sometime before 1858, the family moved to No. 3 Gråbrødre Torv in the center of town. Today it is a pleasant, quiet square, closed to traffic and surrounded by restaurants, cafes, and shops,[21] No. 3 was built in 1769; the ground floor is now occupied by a gift shop. A plaque on the façade of the building states: "[The Danish playwright] Johan Herman Wessel lived here in 1772 when he wrote 'Love Without Stockings.' "[22]

Much of the square (though apparently not No. 3) was destroyed when the British navy bombarded Copenhagen in 1807, during the Napoleonic Wars. When Marcus

Gråbrødre Torv as it appeared in 2001. Marcus and Emma Salomon and their children lived at No. 3, the second house from the left.

Salomon moved there half a century later, it had been rebuilt and the center of the square was occupied by a rather unsightly building that housed several butcher shops. The butcher shops were not removed until 1900.

The birth records of three of Marcus's children who were born in Copenhagen identify their father as either as a manufacturer or a merchant. He probably was both. He opened a shoe shop in Copenhagen soon after his arrival there. In an age when ready-to-wear clothing was far less common than it is today, he almost certainly made shoes for his customers. Marcus continued to have close business ties with northern Germany after his move to Copenhagen. Two of his sons were apprenticed to German merchants in Kiel during the 1870s.

In addition to his own retail shoe business in Copenhagen, Marcus acted as a traveling sales agent for German shoe factories. His sons also became traveling salesmen, selling footwear in Norway and Sweden on behalf of German merchant firms. Thus, Simon, Marcus's youngest son, had traveled extensively in Norway before he decided to settle in that country in the 1890s. While Marcus and his sons were away on business, Emma ran the shop in Copenhagen.

Marcus lived in Denmark for a little over twenty years. In 1879, he and his family moved to Stockholm, where he opened another retail shoe shop.[23] In 1884, he became a Swedish citizen. As a young man living in Stockholm during the 1880s, Simon worked for his father and learned how to make and repair shoes. Within a few years, however, Marcus and Emma left Sweden for good and moved to Hamburg, near Marcus's birthplace of Altona, where he died in 1891.[24]

Sometime during the late 1880s, Simon's older brother Siegmund moved to Oslo and opened a shoemaker's shop there, and Simon joined him in 1893.[25] Both brothers lived in Norway for more than twenty years. Siegmund left Norway in 1913 and lived mostly in Denmark for the remaining thirty years of his life. Simon returned to his native Denmark in 1915, and he died there the following year. Nevertheless, Norway had a strong attraction for the Salomon family. Simon's widow and two of her children went back to live in Norway in the 1920s; and Siegmund's wife and children also returned to live in Norway. Today Simon's grandchildren and *their* grandchildren comprise a numerous Norwegian family.

Carl-Johans Gade, Oslo's main thoroughfare, in 1912.

Norway

———

{1893-1915}

SIMON AND SIEGMUND were among the first Jews to live and work in Norway. During the 1890s, the two brothers established a shoe factory in Oslo which was successful from the start and continued to produce shoes and sporting goods long after the Salomons had ended their connection with it. The brand name Salomon became known throughout Norway.[26]

Norway has a reputation as a liberal, socially progressive country. It is not so well known, however, that Norway has a history of anti-Semitism going back more than two centuries that surfaced virulently during World War II.

From the Middle Ages until the early nineteenth century, Norway was a Danish colony. However, Denmark made the mistake of siding with France and against Britain and her allies during the Napoleonic Wars. The result was a disaster for the Danes. The British navy twice bombarded Copenhagen, doing enormous damage, and captured Denmark's fleet.

After France was defeated in 1814 by Britain and her allies, Denmark was forced to cede Norway to Sweden and Norway and Sweden became a joint kingdom. The union of the two countries, in which Sweden was the dominant power, lasted ninety years.

Despite the union with Sweden, Norway was allowed to control most of its internal affairs and to have its own constitution. In April 1814, 112 of the country's most eminent men met in the town of Eidsvold to adopt a Norwegian constitution. The delegates agreed on a set of ten principles that represented the most liberal and democratic thinking in all of Europe; they guaranteed a constitutional monarchy, representative government, freedom of speech, an independent judiciary, economic freedom, and abolition of the nobility. These principles were embodied in the Norwegian constitution, which was adopted on May 17, 1814, a date still celebrated every year as the country's most important national holiday.[27] However, Article 2 of the Constitution contained the following clause:

> The Evangelical-Lutheran Religion shall be maintained and constitutes the established Church of the Kingdom. The inhabitants who profess the same religion are bound to educate their children in the same. Jesuits and Monastic orders shall not be tolerated. *Jews are furthermore excluded from entering the Kingdom.* [Emphasis supplied.]

The exclusionary clause, stark and uncompromising, is unique in the history of modern democratic constitutions.[28] With the exception of Spain with its long history of extreme Catholicism and the Inquisition, no other European country excluded Jews in the early nineteenth century.[29] On the contrary, several nations, beginning with France during the French Revolution, were at that very time emancipating their Jewish populations from age-old restrictions. In the same year that Norway adopted its constitution, its neighbor Denmark gave civil rights to the Jews.[30]

Norway's decision to exclude Jews from the country did not represent a break with tradition. Even under the Danish kings who ruled Norway until 1814, Jews were not permitted to reside in Norway. They were permitted to visit for short periods, but only if they could obtain a letter from the king.[31]

Surprisingly, most books on Norway's political history, including those written in the twentieth century, unequivocally praise the Norwegian constitution of 1814 but fail to explain or even to comment on the exclusionary clause. *Norwegian Democracy,* for example, published in 1963 by an American scholar, quotes the ten principles underlying the 1814 constitution, including the one stating that "Jews shall be excluded from the kingdom" with no attempt to explain the exclusion. In fact, this author uncritically quotes a British political writer's praise of the constitution: "There is not probably in the history of mankind another instance of a free constitution, not erected amidst ruins and revolution . . . found to be suitable without alteration to all the ends of good government. The reason of this singularity is, that all the essential parts of liberty were already in the country."[32] Apparently, this author (and others) saw no contradiction between devotion to liberty and exclusion of Jews from the country.

Religion was the most important reason for the exclusion clause. Interestingly, the provision was not in the original draft of the constitution, but representatives from the provinces, where the state Lutheran church wielded its most influence, insisted on its inclusion, and it was adopted by a large majority of the delegates to the Eidsvold Convention.[33] If a Jew converted to Christianity, he or she was not excluded.

Lutheranism was the established religion of Norway, and many Norwegians of the nineteenth century took Martin Luther's anti-Semitic teachings seriously. Luther passionately hated the Jews, whom he regarded as greedy blasphemers and murderers. His program for dealing with Jews could have come right out of *Mein Kampf.* He advocated burning down their synagogues, destroying their homes, depriving them of their prayer books, prohibiting their rabbis from teaching under penalty of death, forbidding them to travel, forcing them to earn their living by physical labor, and eventually expelling them from Germany.[34]

Throughout the nineteenth century and earlier, the Lutheran Church exercised enormous power and prestige in Norway. It was a criminal act punishable by imprisonment or a fine to scorn or mock "God's Word or Sacraments" or the official State religion; and, if the act occurred in print, the author could be sentenced to hard labor for life. This law was enforced, and people were severely punished for anti-religious writings.[35]

The exclusionary clause was debated at the Eidsvold Convention. Some representatives argued that it was intolerant, illiberal, and inhumane. The majority, however, supported the clause on religious, political, conservative, and economic grounds. Religious because the Jewish religion was considered barbaric and of little moral value; political, because it was thought that Jews could not be expected to have any national loyalty; conservative, because excluding the Jews simply preserved the status quo; and economic, because it was feared that Jews would be unfair competitors and would obtain great influence over Norwegian business.[36]

Arguably, the fact that the constitutional ban against the Jews also applied to monastic orders and Jesuits indicates that Jews were not the only members of a dissenting religious group singled out for exclusion. But there is an important difference between discriminating against members of a religious order such as the Jesuits and discriminating against all those who adhere to a particular faith or come from a particular background, such as the Jewish people. The 1814 constitution assured freedom of worship for all religious sects but at the same time excluded Jews from the country, a contradiction that can be explained only by the notion that Judaism lay outside the realm of ordinary humanity. There can be little doubt that anti-Semitism, based on ignorance and "an imaginary picture of the Jew,"[37] also played a part, despite (or perhaps because of) the fact that no Jews lived in Norway in 1814 and few Norwegians had ever met a Jew.[38]

The exclusionary clause was rigidly enforced. For example, a Jew who was shipwrecked in Norway in 1817 was arrested as a common criminal and expelled from the country.[39] Efforts to repeal the clause, which required approval by a two-thirds vote in three successive sessions of the Norwegian Storting, or parliament, were repeatedly made by the poet and passionate democrat Henrik Wergeland (whose father had been one of the delegates to the Eidsvold Convention in 1814) and his followers — and repeatedly rejected by the Storting. It was not until 1851, six years after Wergeland's early death, that the clause was finally repealed and Jews were permitted to settle anywhere in the country and become Norwegian citizens.

But Jewish immigrants did not exactly flock to Norway. One or two arrived about 1860.[41] Most of the early arrivals were businessmen who, like the Salomons, came from Denmark or Germany.[42] In 1890, shortly before Simon Salomon arrived in Oslo, there were only 214 Jews in Norway. With immigration from Czarist Russia during the 1890s, this number swelled to 642, but only 136 of these lived in the Oslo area.[43] Thus, when Siegmund and Simon Salomon settled there, they were pioneers of a sort. But Simon was not a stranger in Norway. Although few Jews lived in the country, Jewish traveling salesmen had become a familiar sight in Norwegian towns and villages; during the 1880s and 1890s, Simon was one of them, acting as a selling agent for German shoe manufacturers.

Siegmund, left, and Simon Salomon, the two brothers who owned the Salomon Shoe Factory, in 1901.

rep

Siegmund moved to Oslo in the 1880s and opened a shoemaker's shop in the center of town. When his younger brother Simon joined him in 1893, the two expanded Siegmund's shop into the first shoe factory in Oslo to use industrial methods of production.[44] In the beginning, it was a modest establishment, consisting of a few machines.[45] At the time Siegmund was thirty-five and Simon was thirty-three. Neither was married.

They were well prepared for their endeavor. Both had extensive experience as makers and sellers of shoes, as well as business contacts throughout Norway from their travels as salesmen. Emma, their widowed mother, probably provided part of the capital for the new business, since she and Siegmund were identified as its owners when the business was registered in 1894. Aside from a natural desire to help her sons, Emma may well have believed that the new business was a promising investment for the wealth she had inherited as a result of Marcus's Danish and Swedish ventures. In any event, the Salomon & Son Mechanical Shoe Factory was well financed from its very beginning. Although Simon was identified as business manager (but not an owner), it appears that during most of the years Siegmund and Simon worked together in Oslo it was as partners.[46]

The 1890s was a propitious time to start an industrial business in Norway. Oslo had become an important, thriving commercial port. Knut Hamsun, Norway's greatest novelist (and, incidentally, a notorious anti-Semite), described the city in 1890 as a place where "The ships lay off the piers, the sea was rocking in the sunshine. Everywhere there was busyness, steam whistles shrieking, longshoremen with boxes on their shoulders, cheerful load-

lew

ing songs from the barges."[47] Employment in Norwegian industry increased by 25 percent during the last five years of the nineteenth century. One historian of Norway states:

> It was not until the last three decades of the [nineteenth] century that all the interlocking technical, financial, labour, and transport problems associated with an industrial revolution were brought sufficiently into harmony for an explosive, though uneven, development to take place. . . . During this period industry had advanced on a broad front and naturally it involved change. . . . By 1900 the livelihoods of 27 per cent of the population of Norway depended on some form of industry or associated trades.[49]

This growth was due partly to the development of the country's ample hydroelectric power[50] and partly to its link with Sweden, which permitted free trade between the two countries. Furthermore, Norwegian industrialists of the 1890s were not restricted by many regulations protecting employees. It was not until the first decade of the twentieth century, several years after the shoe factory opened, that Norway began to adopt social welfare measures such as publicly funded unemployment, accident and health insurance, safety regulations in factories, restrictions on child labor, wages-and-hours legislation, and compulsory arbitration of labor disputes. For ambitious entrepreneurs, Norway was a land of opportunity. Salomon & Son was an immediate success and would share in the boom years of Norwegian industry that lasted (despite interruption by a couple of recessions) from 1894 to 1916.

The Salomon Shoe Factory, around 1900.

In 1894 the Salomons moved the factory from its cramped quarters on Lakkeveien to leased premises in a more spacious building on Grænsen Gate, in the center of the city. An 1894-96 trade catalogue advertised the business as the biggest shoe factory in Norway, with 100 workers and sixty machines, and stated: "We recommend our products to all the shoe retailers in Norway!" A contemporary photograph of the factory interior shows dozens of women sitting at side-by-side tables in a long wooden building, working at machines that look somewhat rudimentary to our twenty-first–century eyes but almost certainly were state-of-the-art at the time.

The business was incorporated as a limited liability company in 1897, and the following year its name was changed to Salomon Skofabrik (Salomon Shoe Factory), a name that it retained until it closed in the 1950s, long after the two brothers had ceased to be its owners.[51] In 1898, the Salomon brothers built a larger factory on a site the company purchased on Darres Gate, where it could use the hydroelectric power of the nearby Akers River. In 1905 and again in 1910 they expanded the factory onto adjacent land. The company's business offices were located on Karl Johans Gate, the city's main thoroughfare, which begins at the Royal Palace, passes by the market square, university, principal hotels and shops, parliament), and the National Theater; and ends at the main railroad station. The business office of the Salomon Shoe Factory was located in front of the station.

Shoes made by the Salomon factory were of a higher quality than those of any other local manufacturer. For the first time in Norway, it was possible to buy well made shoes not imported from abroad. In the past, Norwegians who could afford to had bought shoes made in England, France, or Germany. Because the Salomons used improved manufacturing methods, their shoes were expensive, and this made them hard to sell to ordinary Norwegians. To reduce costs, the brothers opened their own retail outlets. Beginning in 1899, the factory had a retail outlet in Oslo, a shoe store named Solid, located across the street from the factory on Graensen Gate. A contemporary photograph of the Solid store shows it to be a large and handsome establishment, with at least four plate-glass windows and the Salomon name prominently displayed. The building, with its distinctive architecture, still stands today. A 1911 newspaper advertisement shows a crude drawing of the Salomon factory and the shoe store, with the caption: "Use Salomon shoes! The country's largest and most fashionable shoe factory. Sales outlet at the shoe store 'Solid.'" The advertisement indicates that the Solid store also sold shoes imported from Paris and Vienna. After a few years, Salomon shoes were sold in Solid stores in several Norwegian cities. According to Siegmund's son, Victor, "In the business, Father was very farsighted and inventive. When the city of Oslo built Homenkolbanen, an electric train that went from the city up to the mountains, he was able to put his brand name on all the poles that held up the electric wires. It created great opposition from the population (early environmental concerns), but all the arguments in the press only created more publicity for the business, and the signs remained."[52]

Solid, the Salomon brothers' retail shoe shop in Oslo, around 1910. The building still houses a retail store.

The Salomon Shoe Factory prospered, and the two brothers prospered with it. In 1907, company assets were appraised for tax purposes at 340,000 kroner, and the business had an income of 40,000 kroner.[53] Although it is difficult to convert these figures into 2006 dollars, a conservative estimate would place the factory's assets at $7 million and its income at $800,000. One thing is clear: within a few years of the factory's opening, both Siegmund and Simon Salomon had become successful and comfortably well-off, if not extremely wealthy.

The Salomon factory had its share of labor problems. Norwegian factory workers had begun organizing in the 1880s, and by the 1890s many workers, including those of the shoe factory, were members of trade unions. A year or so after the Salomon factory opened, the management posted new work regulations (the records do not show what these regulations were), which the newspaper *The Social Democrat* called "an insult to all humanity and existing laws." The result was a three-day strike. The new regulations were revoked after a government inspector found that they did not comply with the country's labor laws.

A more serious labor conflict occurred in 1895, when the factory employed seventy workers. Salomons reduced their employees' weekly wage from sixteen kroner to fourteen kroner. (sixteen kroner in 1895 had the purchasing power of about $325 dollars in 2004). The workers rejected the wage reduction and went to the office of their labor union to discuss what to do about it. Upon their return to the factory, they found the doors locked. The union threatened a boycott of the factory's products, but offered to negotiate on behalf of the workers. The Salomons rejected the offer with an arrogant reply that must have enraged the union: "The word 'boycott' is mentioned but in view of our lack of knowledge of the Norwegian language we beg an explanation of this word." They employed strikebreakers and installed new labor-saving machines. The situation became so ugly that the strikebreakers were in fear of their lives.[54] After seven weeks, during which many of the affected workers had either left the city or taken jobs in other factories, the union conceded defeat, but retaliated by publishing the names and addresses of the strikebreakers in its newspaper. For a time, the Salomon brothers no longer employed organized workers.[55] In another labor dispute in 1904, they resorted to bringing in Jewish strikebreakers from Russia.[56]

Although it is clear that Siegmund and Simon Salomon were tough employers, they had a more progressive side. They formed a committee of management and workers that came up with a plan that provided the workers with financial incentives by giving them shares in the company.[57] The Salomons were among the first employers in Norway to create such a profit-sharing plan. Perhaps, like many industrialists of that era, the Salomons were willing to be benevolently paternalistic toward their employees, but they actively resented any attempt by the government or organized labor to tell them how to run their business. In addition, Siegmund took part in establishing the Union of Norwegian Shoe Factories in 1901, and he was a member of a committee that developed regulations for the Norwegian Shoe Factory Association.

Simon was respected and even loved by many of his employees. Many years later, his granddaughter Frøydis Salomon met a man in Hamar who had worked in the factory. The old shoemaker remembered Simon as a person who treated his workers with kindness and consideration, and also one who taught them to make and repair shoes well. When Simon retired from active management of the factory in March 1915, his administrative staff presented him with a handsome silver bowl with strawberries, leaves, and flowers embossed on it and an engraved inscription: "Simon Salomon. From his staff at the Salomon Shoe Factory."

On November 13, 1896, Simon married. Johanna Bella Eisenstein was one of eleven children of a rabbi who may have come originally from Riga, Latvia. She was born on November 11, 1871, in the town of Plock, in Poland, which was then under Russian rule. Within a year after her birth, the family moved to Dresden in Saxony and became German citizens, most likely because her father was threatened with conscription into the Russian army. Johanna's mother is reputed to have come from a rich Polish family.

Simon met Johanna in Berlin, where she was working as a lady's companion. When Johanna told her parents about the proposed marriage, they were not happy about it, for two reasons: first, Simon lived in Norway and, second, he was not an observant Jew. But when they met him they liked him, and they eventually dropped their objections to the marriage. Johanna was twenty-five at the time of their wedding, eleven years younger than Simon. Johanna accompanied her husband to Oslo in 1896 and three years later both became Norwegian citizens.

The fact that Simon was in Berlin when he met his future wife suggests that he continued to have business connections with Germany even after he and his brother established their shoe factory in Norway. Norwegian records also indicate that, in addition to running the business with his brother, Simon continued his activity as a traveling salesman in rural Norway at least until 1900, on behalf of German companies as well as for his own shoe factory.

Marcus and Emma had practiced the Jewish religion, at least to the extent of keeping a kosher home, but although their son Siegmund became president of the Israelite Congregation in Oslo, neither he nor Simon had much interest in religion. Siegmund's son Victor recollects that he was brought up in a non-Jewish environment and knew nothing about synagogue services.[58] Victor's mother, Melitta, "grew up in a family that for all practical purposes had given up Jewishness." Simon's secularism, however, inevitably created tensions with his wife, Johanna, who as the daughter of a rabbi had grown up in an orthodox home. When Simon proposed to her, she was reluctant to move to Norway, but she relented when Simon assured her that kosher meat was available in Oslo. According to family lore, Simon brought the meat for dinner home with him after he left the factory and told Johanna (untruthfully) that he had bought it at a kosher butcher on the other side of town, where Oslo's Jewish immigrants from Russia and Poland lived.

Another family story illustrates Simon's easygoing attitude toward religion. A friend of his who was a Roman Catholic asked Simon to be the godfather of his child. Simon was delighted to accept, but the priest objected, saying only somebody who had been baptized could be a godfather. So Simon's friend threw a party and baptized Simon with champagne. After the priest was told that Simon been baptized, he permitted him to be the child's godfather.

Despite his indifference to religion, Simon was very

conscious — as well as proud — of being a Jew. It should be remembered that he settled in Oslo shortly before the turn of the century — the time of the Dreyfus Affair in France, which triggered anti-Semitic sentiment throughout Europe. This period also marked the beginning of the Zionist Movement, created by the Viennese journalist Theodore Herzl. Simon's first child was born in Oslo on March 6, 1898, six weeks after the French newspaper *Aurore* published Emile Zola's famous letter that began with the words "J'Accuse," a crushing denunciation of all those who had had a hand in the viciously anti-Semitic persecution of the innocent Captain Dreyfus. "J'Accuse" has been called the most important newspaper article in history.[59] Although Simon's eldest child was always known as Max, his full name was Marcus Zola Salomon. Simon told his son that his middle name honored Emile Zola's courage and integrity. Norwegian law did not permit a child to have a first name that was not on a prescribed list of names, so Zola became Max's middle name.[60]

A few years later, Simon demonstrated publicly his pride in his Jewish origins and his disgust at Norwegian anti-Semitism, which periodically surfaced, eventually with disastrous results for the Norwegian Jews during the German occupation of 1940-45. Although his children and grandchildren married non-Jews and became assimilated into Norwegian and Danish life, Simon did not. Furthermore, he was not the kind of man to accept calumny against the Jews in silence. In 1910, a Norwegian lawyer named Eivind Saxlund wrote a book, *Jews and Goyim,* that was heavily influenced by the German anti-Semitic literature of the day, and its publication led to a debate in various Oslo newspapers. In a letter that was printed on the front page of the newspaper *Tidens Tegn*[61] (*Signs of the Times*) in January 1911, Saxlund replied to a Christian clergyman named Ragnvald Gjessing who had criticized the book. Saxlund claimed that Gjessing was infected by Jewish "chutspah" and repeated his attack on the Jews, their ethics, and their supposed power in Norway. Simon Salomon wrote a long, caustic reply to Saxlund that appeared in the same newspaper (though not on the front page) on February 6, 1911, portions of which are worth quoting because they illustrate Simon's refusal to hide his background or to compromise with anti-Semitism:

> One must be surprised by the naivete you express in your answer to vicar Gjessing. . . . You ask the Jews to defend themselves against the villainous accusations that are flung at them in your book . . ., which by the way is nothing but a copy of certain anti-Semitic scripts.
>
> You do not believe then that the Jews are so childish that they would help you with a cheap advertisement for your trashy book. But since the advertisement is already done, I suppose it doesn't make any difference whether you sell a few copies more or less of your lampoon.
>
> You accuse vicar Gjessing of being infected by 'chutspah.' But it is hard to find a greater 'chutspah' than yours, since you have copied word-for-word from German anti-Semitic scripts all those lies German money-blackmailers have invented about the Jews.
>
> . . .

It wouldn't hurt you to learn about Jewish ethics. Such a study would certainly do you good, and your morals would probably improve considerably.

Your fear that the Jews will become a danger for Norway is groundless, according to my knowledge. I know only one Jewish man who has earned a small fortune here in Norway. That was the trader Vollman in Frankfurt am Main, who passed away a couple of weeks ago. He didn't forget that he made his money here, since he at his death left 50,000 kroner to the poor in Oslo. Was this a result of Jewish ethics? Thirty years after the man left the country, he hadn't forgotten about Norway and the city where he made his money.

. . .

In your answer to vicar Gjessing you say that you would have been glad to read an objective confrontation. You demand something quite impossible: One cannot confront in writings – using your own lovely words – 'all the hatred, bitterness, poison, gall, and hostility towards mankind and the evil spirit of persecution' that your script contains. Only a mentally retarded person would engage in a confrontation about your script of shame.

What eventually made me show any interest at all in you was the statement that this publication was motivated by the love for your compatriots. I do not believe it. You don't need love to press your compatriots for 1.50 kroner for your trashy book. Books of this kind are now displayed in Berlin, in the so-called pulp fiction shelf, and they are sold for only 10 pfennigs each. It would have been a little proof of your idealistic purpose if you gave the profit of the sales to the poor in Oslo.

This is my first, and my last, newspaper article about this matter; I won't create more advertising for your book.

Simon and Johanna had five children: Marcus Zola (Max), born in 1898; Gjertrud (Gerda), born in 1899; Harald, born in 1900; Margaret (Grete, my mother), born in 1901; and Alfred, born in 1904. For the children, Oslo in the first years of the twentieth century was close to paradise. There was skiing, sledding, and skating in the winter, and swimming and boating on Oslo Fjord in the summer. Although Oslo in 1901 had a population of 230,000, it did not have a big-city atmosphere. Edvard Munch described the city at this period: "The center still has a small-town look about it. Only parts of East Oslo, with the long streets and the rows of tenement blocks, smack of a big city in appearance and atmosphere."

Oslo is one of the northernmost cities of the world, but its climate, affected by the Gulf Stream, is fairly moderate. Here is how Munch's brother Andreas, writing to him from Norway in May 1894, described Oslo:

As early as mid-March spirea and honeysuckle had started to flower and I regularly saw larks and butterflies. Ever since then I've been able to work with the windows open in the middle of the day. Yesterday, the first leaves on the chestnuts were out and one cherry tree is a mass of blossom. Apart from this, the trees are bare, but with buds ready to come out. The lawns are green. At midday it was as high as

16 degrees [Celsius] in the shade. Karl Johans Gade is lovely in the daytime. When the orchestra plays there are masses of brightly-coloured clothes and gaudy parasols.[62]

In summer, many Oslo residents, including the Salomons, rented cottages on the small islands in Oslo fjord or on a wooded peninsula that juts into the fjord. An early-twentieth century English traveler wrote about the fjord in summer:

Each of these little islands seemed a paradise in its way — delightfully idyllic little places, well-wooded and cool-looking. Everywhere people were bathing — from boats, from the shore, and from miniature bathing-houses. Here was yet another side of [Oslo's] many-sided life; truly its inhabitants are a fortunate people![63]

When Simon's children were old enough, they would row him to work in town in the mornings and pick him up in the rowboat in the evening. The cottage must have been very near the city, for on one such occasion, when Gerda was nine and Grete seven, the boys rowed him into town in the morning, and the girls rowed him home in the afternoon. Both girls were wearing red dresses. After Gerda had rowed part of the way, her younger sister said she wanted to row. When Gerda wouldn't let her, Grete stood up in the boat and angrily insisted on rowing. In her eagerness, she tipped the boat over and they both ended up in the fjord. The dye of their red dresses ran, all over them. When Simon met them at the dock, he laughed and said that they were not his daughters but two red fish.

During the early years of the century, when Simon's five children were growing up, the family lived in an apartment house at No. 11 Geitemyrsveien, a residential street facing the park of St. Hanshaugen (St. John's Hill). The building is now used as a women's residence. Sometime after 1905, however, they moved to a splendid white stucco house with a large garden, further up the hill at No. 27B. Even today, the house (now divided into apartments) is impressive in its beauty, with its terra-cotta tile roof, doric columns, and surrounding shrubbery.[64] The big garden is gone, however — land in Oslo having become more and more valuable — and a nondescript modern house stands where it once grew.

Kristiania. Gjetemyrsveien

Gjetemyrsveien, Oslo, around 1910. This is where Grete Salomon lived as a young girl. (Courtesy of Oslo City Museum)

No. 27B Gjetemyrsveien, the family's home as it appeared in 2004.

A century ago, when there were very few automobiles and houses were spaced well apart, each with its own garden surrounding it, St. Hanshaugen must have been an ideal place for young children to grow up. Many years later, Grete liked to tell us about her childhood there, much of the time in the outdoors, often bicycling or sledding down the long hill on Geitemyrsveien. St. Hanshaugen was also a popular pleasure resort, with a park, a public promenade, restaurants, and cafes. From there, one could see the entire city and the fjord. Further out was Holmenkollen, already Norway's most famous ski resort, with an even more spectacular view of the city.

In 1905, war threatened when Norway attempted to dissolve its century-old union with Sweden. But the Swedes agreed to a peaceful end to the union, and Norway became, for the first time since the Middle Ages, a completely independent nation. There was general rejoicing in Oslo, in which the Salomon family must have participated, although the children were probably still too young (Max, the oldest, was seven, and Alfred, the youngest, was one) to fully appreciate the significance of the event.

Nine years later, on May 17, 1914, less than three months before World War I began, Norway celebrated the hundredth anniversary of its constitution. By that time, the Salomon children were old enough to enjoy the elaborate festivities. There was a great exhibition in the Oslo suburb of Frogner, where buildings, flower gardens, lakes, waterfalls, stately promenades, and secret paths had been created for the occasion. There were restaurants and musical events there too.

Although the Salomon family lived within Oslo, the children led a largely outdoor, carefree life. Grete, the only child of Simon and Johanna to live most of her life outside Scandinavia, always looked back at her Norwegian childhood with a deep, piercing nostalgia. During our own childhood, she would regale us with stories of growing up in Oslo. She fell off her bicycle and broke a tooth riding down the long hill where the family lived; she bit into an apple and found half a worm inside; and so on. She told these stories, and others, time and again.

Gerda too, who lived in the United States from 1941 until the end of her long life, regarded Norway as the Kingdom of Heaven, according to her son-in-law, Lloyd Berg. And Johanna and her two oldest children, Max and Gerda, loved Norway so much that they returned there in the 1920s after living several years in Denmark. Similarly, Siegmund's wife and children left Denmark to live in Norway after the First World War.

Often, the good old days exist only in memory, but there is every reason to believe that the Salomon children had a pretty wonderful childhood. In large part this was due to their father, who, by all accounts, was a man of understanding, humor, and tolerance. Johanna, on the other hand, had an authoritarian personality and a propensity to dominate the lives of her children, without, however, providing them with sensible or helpful guidance. One can guess that the children went to their father for relief from their mother's rigidity. His death in 1916, at 55, when his children were still teenagers, must have been an unimaginable tragedy for the entire family. Strangely, in later life Grete seldom talked about him; his loss must have been so difficult that she suppressed all thought of him. Similarly, there is not a single mention of Simon in letters Johanna wrote to her children during and after the war.

Siegmund, Simon's partner and older brother, did not marry until 1899, when he was forty-one. His wife, Melitta Rosenthal, came from Lübeck, in northern Germany. She was twenty years younger than her husband. The couple had six children: Anny, born in 1900; Hans, born in 1901; Willy (known as Jarl), born in 1903; Marcus Victor, born in 1905; Elly, born in 1910; and Sven, born in 1915. Anny died of meningitis in 1916, while the family was living in Germany. Jarl and Marcus emigrated to the United States in 1940, where they changed their names to Jarl Norman and Victor Norman. Hans and Elly were living in Norway when the Germans invaded the country in 1940.

Simon's stay in Norway and the Salomon brothers' operation of their shoe factory lasted only about two decades. In 1913, Siegmund retired from the business and sold his house in Oslo with the intention of moving his family to a warmer climate. For four years, they lived in Germany and then, owing to wartime privations in that country, returned to Denmark. After the war, Siegmund resumed his traveling habit, in part because he loved to travel but also to avoid Danish taxes, which included a tax on capital as well as on income. If he stayed nine months or more of the year outside Denmark, he could avoid these taxes. Because his wife, Melitta, did not enjoy traveling, Siegmund usually went alone or with one or more of his children.[65] Eventually, he returned to Copenhagen, where he lived until his death in 1943, at the age of eighty-five.

Simon did not stay in Norway much longer than his brother. He retired from the business around March 1915 and returned to his birthplace of Copenhagen, where he died of cancer on June 3, 1916. Even though retired, Simon remained a director of the Salomon Shoe Factory until his death, after which Siegmund took his place on the board until 1925. Evidently, the Salomons retained a financial interest in the business even after their active participation in it had ended.

It is not clear whether Simon retired and moved with his family to the milder climate and more cosmopolitan and tolerant atmosphere of Copenhagen because of his illness, or whether he became ill after his retirement and before the move. His daughter, Grete, firmly believed that it was because Simon no longer had an occupation that he was afflicted by cancer, the lesson being that a person who remains active stays healthy in both body and mind. It is also possible that Simon and Johanna felt that their two daughters would have better opportunities to find suitable (i.e., Jewish) husbands in Denmark, which, unlike Norway, had a substantial upper-middle-class Jewish population.

The tombstone of Emma Salomon in the Sofienberg Jewish cemetery in Oslo. Note that the inscription is in German. A Hebrew inscription is on the other side.

Another possible reason for their departure from Norway was the outbreak of war in Europe in August 1914. Although Norway remained neutral, it was profoundly affected by the war. Hostilities brought widespread fear of food and fuel shortages because Norway depended on supplies from abroad. During the first week of the war, there was panic in Oslo, hoarding of supplies, breaking of shop windows, and riots that had to be suppressed by the police. Because Norway relied on the British navy to keep the sea lanes open and because German submarines sank Norwegian ships and killed Norwegian sailors, Norwegians tended to be pro-British and anti-German. As a Jew married to a German wife, Simon may have felt that Denmark would provide the family with a more agreeable atmosphere than Norway

Whether as a result of the war, Simon's illness, Norwegian anti-Semitism, or for other reasons, in 1915 Simon and Johanna and their five children, then eleven to eighteen years old, moved to Copenhagen, which became the family's home for the next eight years.

An undated photo of Johanna Salomon with her daughters Gerda, left, and Grete.

The Years Between
the Wars

———

WHEN SIMON AND JOHANNA SALOMON and their five children arrived in Denmark in 1915, they moved into a large handsome brick house at 14 Gersonvej in the Copenhagen suburb of Hellerup. Simon died of cancer the following year, leaving enough money for Johanna to live comfortably — although not in great luxury — during the forty years of her widowhood, and in addition to educate her children and occasionally to make substantial gifts to them. The family lived in the house in Hellerup until 1923, when Johanna returned to Norway.

Although the children, approaching adulthood in 1916, had enjoyed Oslo's outdoor life, pleasure-loving, well-fed, gracious Denmark may have been a relief after the austerity of wartime Norway. According to a book written at about the time of the family's move to Denmark, "The social life of the Danes, particularly in the metropolis, has in recent years undergone a notable change, developing very much along French lines. Café, salon and restaurant habits are increasing in a pronounced manner. Despite these facts, however, the Danes still remain a charming and hospitable people."[66]

Thirty years later, when Johanna was once more living in Copenhagen after World War II, she described vividly to her daughters a party (she called it a fairy tale) that reminded her of the Danish graciousness and hospitality that she first had enjoyed there during and immediately after the First World War:

> Harald and I were invited to Jørgen Palsbøl's for a big dinner. There were a lot of young people there, since they have three daughters aged 14-18 years and a thirteen year old son. . . . [Jørgen's wife] is in her 40s. You have no idea how nice these people are; you really feel that both of them only want to make you feel as comfortable as possible.
>
> Jørgen's mother and sister were also present. First we had a lovely meal followed by coffee and cognac, liquor, and cigars. Then plenty of fruit, apples, oranges, pears, caramelized almonds, marzipan, the first available chocolate and soda, seltzer water, etc. Then we saw a slide show that lasted for hours, and there was tea and an abundance of cakes. By then, it was already 12:30 a.m., and then J. gave us – meaning his mother, his sister and myself – a ride home in his car. I haven't partied like that since you girls were here with me.

It is quite likely that Johanna was among those who enjoyed a cigar at the party; in the 1940s, visitors to Denmark were often surprised to see that it was a special custom among Danish women to smoke cigars; and it seems clear that Johanna, then seventy-four, entered fully into the spirit of the party.

The house in Hellerup, outside Copenhagen, where Johanna and her children lived from 1915 to 1923.

Despite her enjoyment of parties and good food, Johanna was an unhumorous and on the whole unimaginative person. Moreover, as long as she was able to, she tried to control the lives of her children. Although there is no evidence that she was an observing Jew, she was implacably hostile to the idea that any of them might marry a Gentile. She refused to attend the weddings of any of her three sons, all of whom married outside the Jewish faith (Max and Alfred each did so twice). Unsurprisingly, she was not on good terms with her daughters-in law, particularly Harald's wife, Else.

Although Johanna could not control her sons' choice of wives, she exercised an inflexible veto over her two daughters' choice of husbands. This was in an age and social culture where a young upper middle-class woman had but one approved purpose in life: to find a husband. To Johanna, any prospective son-in-law had to meet only two requirements, but they were inflexible: first, he had to be Jewish and, second, he had to be a businessman. Both daughters complied with Johanna's wishes, with unfortunate consequences. Their husbands were probably far less suitable than any they themselves would have chosen without maternal pressure. Gerda was twice married and twice quickly divorced. Grete's marriage lasted thirty-three years, but it was far from happy. It is of course impossible to say how Gerda and Grete's lives would have turned out if their father had not died when they were adolescents; but this liberal, intelligent, and tolerant man might have given them the guidance and support they needed during their early adulthood.

In 1923, Johanna returned to Norway, where she had lived during most of the twenty years of her marriage and where all her children had been born. For the next seventeen years, she lived in a small chalet-like house in Voksenlia, a pretty town in the hills outside Oslo. During most of those years, her son Max, then a widower, and her daughter Gerda, who was divorced, lived nearby.

Because Max was Simon and Johanna's oldest son, they expected him to become a businessman. According to his elder daughter, Frøydis, this was "very unfortunate since that was one thing he absolutely was not." Originally, Simon may have wanted Max to work with him in the shoe factory in Norway and eventually take it over, but that plan ended when Simon retired from the business and the family moved to Denmark. Max was seventeen at the time. A few years later, Max fell in love with Olga Swanholm, a beautiful Danish girl from a wealthy non-Jewish family. In order to separate the pair, Johanna, now a widow, persuaded Max to go abroad for a year. Max worked in the United States for Standard Oil of New Jersey (since renamed Exxon) during 1920 and 1921.

Max returned from the United States and married Olga without his mother's blessing. A snapshot, taken around the time of the marriage shows Olga in affectionate repose with Max, standing close to him, her left arm draped over his shoulder. Six months later, she was dead of tuberculosis, a disease so prevalent at the time that it has been called "the scourge of Denmark."[67] Frøydis, the elder daughter of Max's second marriage, calls Olga her father's "life-love" and says that Max "never quite got over her death, and it seems he sort of lacked some life-confidence ever after."

Max and his first wife, Olga Swanholm, around 1922.

Max in Brooklyn around 1921.

Not long after Olga's death, Max joined his mother in Norway, which remained his home for the rest of his life. For several years, he lived in the hilly countryside outside Oslo with a large German shepherd dog named Leo as his only companion — first in Holmenkollen, now famous for its ski jump and as the site of the 1952 Winter Olympic Games, and later in nearby Voksenlia.

In Norway, Max tried his hand at various endeavors, apparently without success. During the 1920s, he managed a shoe store in Oslo, a position that he no doubt owed to his late father's and his uncle Siegmund's connections. Later he was a sales representative for an advertising firm, and in 1928 this work took him on another visit to the United States. During most of the years between the two world wars, however, Max worked in the fur business, to which he had first been introduced by the father-in-law from his short-lived marriage. Although Max did not inherit Simon's business abilities, he did inherit many of his father's personal qualities. Like Simon, he had a good sense of humor and tended to be friendly and tolerant. He was a public-spirited man; ironically, it took the war and exile from Norway to enable his escape from a career in business and allow his engagement in the kind of work for which he was best suited.

Although Max was born in Norway and lived there most of his life, he somehow felt himself to be an outsider because he was Jewish. Unlike his younger brother Harald, who was tall and fair-haired and looked like most people's idea of a typical Scandinavian, Max was of medium height and had dark hair and a swarthy complexion. Like many Scandinavian Jews, Max did not want to be Jewish. Soon after the war, he told one of his nephews that his experience during the war, requiring him to flee Norway and live in exile in Sweden for five years, had caused him to give up any identity as a Jew.

Around 1936 or 1937, Max married Nora Philippina Herz, who came from a wealthy German family of Jewish origin that had converted to Lutheranism long before she was born. The family owned a jewelry business in Berlin. Nora's parents had named her after the heroine of Henrik Ibsen's *A Doll's House;* her name was singularly prophetic, in view of her independent spirit and her destiny to live most of her life in Norway. In the early 1930s she moved to London in order to escape her parents' control and became a schoolteacher. There she met Max, who was working in London. After the wedding, Max and Nora settled in Oslo, but Nora refused to live in Voksenlia near her domineering mother-in-law. She insisted on moving to the opposite end of Oslo, the suburb of Nordstrand on the high eastern shore of Oslo Fjord, where the couple bought a large frame house with a spectacular view of the fjord.[68] Frøydis, their oldest child, was born there shortly before the beginning of World War II. The family was living in Nordstrand on April 9, 1940, when the Germans invaded Norway.

Gerda, Johanna's second child, was married at twenty-one to a German traveling salesman whom Johanna picked out for her. For a short time, the couple lived in style in an apartment in post-World War I Berlin. However, the marriage was a disappointment because Gerda seldom saw her husband, whose work required him to spend much of his time traveling in the Baltic states. The marriage ended within a year or two. Johanna, who continued to be deeply involved in managing (or trying to manage) her children's lives, helped Gerda get her divorce.

After the divorce, Gerda returned to Norway. For several years, she lived a comfortable and uneventful life of leisure, made possible by her father's estate, and perhaps supplemented by alimony. In 1933, she married Siegfried Weill, who had been born in England and was a British subject, but who lived in Berlin. Her second marriage lasted only about three years. The couple separated soon after the birth of their daughter Dorrit, and Gerda again returned to Norway. With Hitler in power, Siegfried returned to England, where he served in the British Army during the war. Although Gerda's marriage to Siegfried was dissolved, she retained her British passport. She was

Gerda (front row, extreme right) on the gala night of a Mediterranean cruise in 1925.

*Gerda and Siefgried Weill on their honeymoon
at Westgate-on-Sea, England, in 1933.*

living with her daughter in an apartment in Oslo in 1940 when Hitler's forces invaded Norway. She was forty-one years of age. Nothing up to that time had prepared her for the challenges she then faced, but she met these challenges with intelligence, courage, and decisiveness.

The fifty-year marriage of Harald, Johanna's third child, to Else Magnussen, the daughter of a Danish art dealer, was happy and stable. It ended only with Else's death in 1975. Harald was a tall, handsome, and impressive man. His Norwegian niece Frøydis wrote about him: "He was a very broad-minded, easy-going person, and I liked him very much." Harald had a fortunate and productive life, marred only by the harrowing experience of his escape from Denmark with his family in October 1943.

Because Harald was not the oldest son, Johanna did not try to force him into business, although she disapproved of his career as an artist. Soon after the family moved to Copenhagen, Harald had begun his artistic education. In 1922, he was admitted to the Royal Danish Academy of Fine Arts, where he studied sculpture until 1927. After Johanna returned to Norway in 1923, Harald continued his sculpture studies in Denmark, and in 1927 he became a Danish citizen.

In the same year, Harald joined the Royal Danish Mint as assistant medalist and apprentice to medalist Gunnar Jensen. When Jensen retired in 1933, Harald became medalist of the Mint, a post he held (except during his exile to Sweden in 1943-45) until he retired in 1968. According to one authority, "his simple and tautly composed 1-krone coin from 1942, containing the portrait of [King] Christian X, has been praised as a masterpiece that influenced postwar coins in Denmark."[69] His medals include one made in 1970 to honor David Ben-Gurion (with a menorah on the reverse side), which has been described as bearing "a clear physical resemblance to the sitter";[70] a medal honoring Niels Bohr; and a silver medal showing the great Danish storyteller Hans Christian Andersen on one side and the storyteller's "ugly duckling" on the reverse.

Although Harald seems to have had little interest in the Jewish religion, these three medals suggest that, like his father, who was outspoken in his attack on Norwegian anti-Semitism, he was proud of his Jewish identity. Ben-Gurion was one of the founders, and the first prime minister, of the State of Israel; Bohr, a Nobel Prize laureate and one of the greatest atomic physicists of the twentieth century, was half-Jewish and also played a role (albeit minor) in persuading the Swedish government to give shelter to the Danish Jews in 1943; and the great storyteller Andersen, although not Jewish himself, had close ties to influential Danish Jewish families and spent the last days of his life as a guest in the home of Moritz and Dorothea Melchior, a Jewish couple who were reputed to be the richest commoners in Denmark.[71]

Harald earned a formidable reputation as a sculptor. According to Else Rasmussen, the author of the definitive book on his life and work:

> His most famous art works in Denmark include the decoration of Copenhagen City Hall, the King's Portal at the Christiansborg Castle, and his most outstanding work, the Gephion Fountain located in the port of Copenhagen. He was greatly influenced by the national style, both in terms of subject matter and choice of material, often looked to medieval times for inspiration, and had a preference for working in granite. Moreover, he had a talent for creating narrative sculpture with a clear and comprehensible content. [72]

Harald and Else moved easily in the upper reaches of Danish society, where talent and style were more important than wealth in gaining acceptance. A contemporary account described the Danish meritocracy:

> There is practically no recognition of 'grades' in society. Sets – artistic, literary, theatrical, political – are inevitable in any organised social system, and they are of course to be found in Denmark, with this

Harald Salomon as a young man.

Harald and Else as a young couple.

essential difference, that when seeking admission to
them, birth or position count for nothing and
cleverness for everything.[73]

Harald thrived in this environment. His biographer
sums up his character and life perfectly:

As an artist and as a human being, Harald Salomon
lived on the sunny side of life. Salomon was a
handsome and very charming man, and he was
blessed to find for a wife Else (née Magnussen),
whose strikingly beautiful features throughout the

stages of her life he depicted on medals and busts. Through his in-laws, Salomon gained entrance to Copenhagen's wealthy bourgeoisie, where his family found their friends and acquaintances.[74]

Grete, Simon and Johanna's fourth child, married Jack Poser, the fourth of six sons of Isaac Poser, a wealthy Jewish fur dealer from Cracow. Jack lived in Denmark during the First World War in order to escape military service in the Austrian army. After their marriage, Jack and Grete moved to London, where they lived until 1939, when they moved to New York.

Alfred, the youngest child of Simon and Johanna Salomon, was born on July 24, 1904. I know less about him than about any of his brothers or sisters. Like his brother Harald, he remained in Denmark when other members of the family returned to Norway in the 1920s. For most of his life, Alfred suffered from mental illness, and he was

Jack Poser and Grete on the beach at Hornbaek, Denmark, around 1918.

Gerda and Grete with Joe, around 1926.

institutionalized several times for psychosis and paranoid obsessive thoughts and behavior. As a young man, he moved from one occupation to another, always with unrealistic expectations of success. Sometimes he went on uncontrollable spending sprees, and several times Johanna had to help him financially.

The approach of World War II increased Alfred's mental instability. He became obsessed about the German persecution of the Jews and believed that the Germans were spying on him. In October 1939, he was hospitalized in Roskilde, the medieval capital city of Denmark located about 20 miles from Copenhagen, in whose ancient cathedral the Danish kings are buried. He was a patient at Roskilde Hospital when the Germans invaded the country.

Siegmund, Simon's older brother and partner, retired

Joe, Norman, and Liz, Westgate-on-Sea, around 1936.

from active management of the Salomon Shoe Factory in 1913. With his wife, Melitta, and their six children (the youngest, Sven, was born after they left Norway), he lived in the German city of Wiesbaden and later in Hamburg. In 1917, Siegmund and his family returned to his native Denmark and bought a large house in Ordrup, a suburb of Copenhagen. After the war, Siegmund resumed his travels in Germany and Switzerland, usually unaccompanied by his wife.

Although Siegmund had retired, he continued to have an interest in a shoe store in Oslo. (It is not clear whether this was the "Solid" store, which Siegmund and Simon had started, or another store Siegmund bought or established.) During the 1920s, two of his sons, Victor and Jarl, returned to Oslo as co-managers of the store, which they operated profitably. Norway continued to hold an attraction to Siegmund's children, who took full advantage of opportunities for skiing in the winter, and mountain climbing and boating in the summer. In 1928, Victor and Jarl returned to Copenhagen, where their father helped them start a wholesale shoe business with their older brother Hans.

But a business career held little attraction either for Victor or Jarl. Both wanted to be musicians: Victor's ambition was to be a conductor, and Jarl's to be a singer. Around 1930, Victor gave up his interest in the Copenhagen shoe business in order to devote himself to the study of music. He graduated from the Danish Royal Music Conservatory in 1932, majoring in conducting.[75] During the next few years he studied and performed in England, France, Austria, and Italy. Jarl spent five years studying to become an operatic singer, and he began to appear in some provincial European opera houses.[76]

In February 1940, Victor sailed for New York on a Norwegian-American liner, and a month later Jarl followed him there on the last transatlantic ship to leave Norway before the German invasion. The two brothers quickly learned that there was plenty of anti-Semitism in the United States; when they visited the New Jersey shore and said their name was Salomon they found that no accommodations were available. On the advice of the conductor Efrem Kurtz, to whom they had an introduction when they arrived in America, they changed their last names, so that from then on they were known as Victor Norman and Jarl Norman.[77]

In January 1941, Victor moved to New London, Connecticut, to become a piano teacher. There, he founded the Eastern Connecticut Symphony Orchestra, which he conducted for thirty-five years until he retired at the age of 75. After his retirement, he established the National Senior Symphony, composed of elderly musicians, which he conducted until his ninetieth year. He also worked for several years at the Electric Boat Division of General Dynamics Corp, which built submarines. Victor Norman died in 2001, at ninety-six. His brother, Jarl, became a concert singer of classical music, and a translator and writer.

Siegmund and Melitta's oldest son, Hans, and their younger daughter, Elly, returned to Norway during the interwar years. Hans remained in the shoe business, living in the Valdres, a rural area in southern Norway, about two-and-a-half hours travel from Oslo; his sister worked as a secretary in Oslo. They both were in Norway when the Germans invaded in 1940.

「Escape」

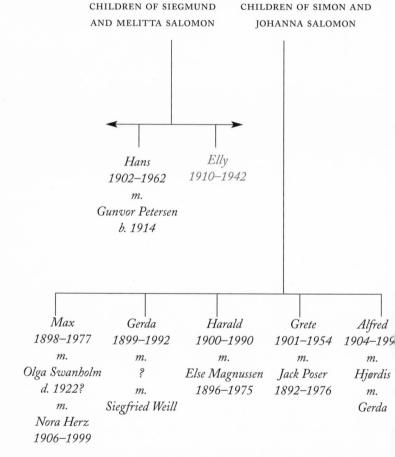

CHILDREN OF SIEGMUND
AND MELITTA SALOMON

CHILDREN OF SIMON AND
JOHANNA SALOMON

Hans
1902–1962
m.
Gunvor Petersen
b. 1914

Elly
1910–1942

Max
1898–1977
m.
Olga Swanholm
d. 1922?
m.
Nora Herz
1906–1999

Gerda
1899–1992
m.
?
m.
Siegfried Weill

Harald
1900–1990
m.
Else Magnussen
1896–1975

Grete
1901–1954
m.
Jack Poser
1892–1976

Alfred
1904–199
m.
Hjørdis
m.
Gerda

The Holocaust Comes
to Scandinavia

{1940-1945}

WHEN THE GERMANS INVADED NORWAY on April 9, 1940, the Norwegian army at first made little attempt to resist. Perhaps unaware that Norwegian shore batteries had sunk the German cruiser *Blücher* in Oslo Fjord and prevented the invading fleet from reaching Oslo, the king, his ministers, and members of the Norwegian parliament left the city before a single German soldier had landed on Norwegian soil. Oslo was left open and undefended, and the city was taken by a small contingent of German soldiers who arrived later that morning at the Oslo airport, which, inexplicably, the Norwegian army did not attempt to defend. By the evening of the invasion, German troops were in full control of Oslo. That evening, Vidkun Quisling, the leader of Nasjonal Samling (NS), Norway's pro-Nazi party, announced on the radio that he was forming a government and told Norwegians not to offer any resistance to the Germans.

Brushing aside Quisling's attempt to form a pro-Nazi independent Norwegian government, Hitler forced Quisling to resign and in late April sent an old-line Nazi, Josef Terboven, as Reichskommisar to rule Norway directly.

Terboven, who had been Gauleiter of Essen, was a "short, thin, humorless man with an icily cold manner." He was personally appointed by Hitler, to whom he reported directly.[78] Terboven quickly abandoned any thought of ruling Norway through a civilian Norwegian government because the major political parties refused to accept Quisling as prime minister. Although Terboven would later allow Quisling to head a puppet government, the German Reichskommisar held the ultimate authority in Norway throughout the war, an authority that he exercised ruthlessly.

In Norway, the Germans found fertile ground for their anti-Jewish program. Anti-Semitism was never far below the surface of Norwegian life. Norway was a harsh, poverty-stricken country during most of the nineteenth century, where everyday life was plagued by the ever-present scourges of tuberculosis, diphtheria, influenza, and alcoholism. Of course this was true of other European countries as well; but the works of two of Norway's greatest artists, the playwright Henrik Ibsen and the painter Edvard Munch, amply depict Norway's deep-rooted strain of fundamentalism, which often led to bigotry, depression, dogmatism, and hysteria. A friend of Munch once tried to describe the two-sided Norwegian character in a letter to the great Norwegian painter:

> I can't understand what it is about the Norwegians, who are one of the finest peoples on earth, one of the cleverest and most talented and at the same time, in a way, so weak, so wild, so lawless. I don't mean lawless in the usual sense, for one ought to break the laws one has created oneself, but there are natural laws, basic

laws and it is just these laws that the Norwegians break and that's why they become so unhappy and hysterical.[79]

There was a wave of anti-Semitism during the 1914-18 war, partly because the public identified Jews with Germany and partly because in a time of shortages prices rose much more rapidly than wages and it was inevitable that Jewish businessmen would be accused of war profiteering. Furthermore, Norwegian hysteria against German spies fixed on the Jews, many of whom were of German origin. A wartime Norwegian police official wrote this about the Jews to the Ministry of Justice: "They are a people without patriotic sentiment, even if they have resided in Norway for many years; they think only of business deals and making money, regardless of the degree of respectability or even legality involved."[80]

With the inconsistency typical of anti-Semitism, some Norwegians also thought that Jews, particularly those who came from Russia and Poland, were revolutionary Bolsheviks. During the war, several thousand Jewish refugees who had fled from Russian pogroms crossed Norway on their way to America, and some of them settled in Norway to earn their living by becoming peddlers. The Norwegian authorities considered these people to be dishonest, unfair competitors who lacked national feeling. In 1917, Norway amended its immigration law to make it more restrictive. Although the law applied to all foreigners, it primarily affected Jews, who found it more difficult to obtain residence and work permits than other immigrant groups.[81]

In the 1930s, as Nazi Germany gained in power and influence, there was another wave of anti-Semitism in Norway. In 1932, the local authorities of an Oslo suburb officially excluded Jews from a resort island in Oslo Fjord without a dissenting vote. A rash of anti-Semitic posters, flyers, and newspaper advertisements appeared. There was even a Norwegian periodical called *Nasjonalt Tidskrift (National Journal)*, whose only purpose was to attack the Jews and all things Jewish; its editor also issued a publication called "Who's Who in the Jewish World" in order to warn Norwegians against coming into contact with Jews.[84] Anti-Semitic feeling ran so high that the owner of an Oslo clothing factory deemed it necessary to disassociate himself from any possible taint of Jewishness by placing the following advertisement in a newspaper on December 1, 1938:

> Announcement: Given that my company's signs and posters have lately been vandalized and rubberstamped with the following statement: "Norwegians, do business with your fellow countrymen, not with Jews," I deem it necessary – in order to avoid any misunderstandings – to notify the public of the fact that the undersigned, Olaf Røsberg, sole proprietor and founder in 1929 of the Storgatens Clothing Factory, is of old Norwegian peasant stock, and so *is not Jewish*.

> "Moreover, in my service – among my approximately 250 factory workers and clerks – there is not a single Jew."[85]

The evident belief of the factory owner that he would be commended rather than condemned by members of the public for placing such a scurrilous advertisement in a newspaper, as well as the willingness of the newspaper to print the advertisement, show the strength of anti-Semitism in Norway even before the war and Nazi occupation. The Danish Consul in Oslo evidently thought the advertisement sufficiently indicative of Norwegian anti-Semitic sentiment to pass it on to his Foreign Office.

After the German invasion of Norway, the Nazi process of destroying the Norwegian Jews followed a pattern similar to that in Germany after Hitler's coming to power, although it happened at a much faster pace — two and a half years (April 1940 to October 1942) in Norway, versus about eight years (1933 to 1941) in Germany. This process involved, first, restricting Jews' rights of citizenship and their ability to earn a living; second, isolating them from the general community; third, confiscating their property and depriving them of their livelihood; and, finally, after this process had dehumanized them in the eyes of much of the population, deporting them and depriving them of their lives.[86] In Norway, few Christian Norwegians took any action to interfere with the process of destroying the Jews. Moreover, the police and civil authorities fully cooperated with the Germans in executing it. According to one historian of the Holocaust in Norway:

> Experienced civil servants and police officers
> understood that the seizure of the Jews' radios and
> property, the stamping of passports, and the arrests
> followed by confiscation of bank books and passports
> were all leading to something unthinkable. That is

why some took pains to warn Jews of forthcoming arrests. Norway was a small country, and the police community and the civil service were even smaller. Jewish persecution could not be kept secret even from those who had no direct involvement.[87]

On May 10, 1940, only a month after the invasion, the German authorities ordered the Norwegian police to confiscate all radios belonging to Jews.[88] The police obeyed the order without protest; they entered Jewish homes and seized the radios. Only a few local police chiefs refused to obey the order.[89] The Norwegian Administrative Council, the highest Norwegian authority in occupied Norway, may have been troubled by this first overt action against Norwegian Jews but they decided not to complain.[90] At about the same time, the Norwegian police required Jewish communities to give up their membership lists, a step that facilitated the subsequent steps of depriving the Jews of their rights and eventually of arresting and deporting them.

In early 1941, members of the Hirden, a Norwegian military organization that patterned itself on the German SS, painted anti-Semitic slogans on Jewish stores in Oslo, and there were a few occasions when Norwegian Nazis smashed the windows of Jewish-owned stores. The NS party of Vidkun Quisling lost no opportunity to make verbal and written attacks on the Jews. In June 1941, all stateless Jewish men (i.e., persons who had lost their citizenship as a result of Nazi persecution) living in Norway were arrested and sent to Norwegian concentration camps. The prisoners from the northern part of the country were held until November 1942, when they were deported to Auschwitz; but those from southern Norway were released after three weeks, only to be arrested again the following year. In August 1941, the Danish Consul in Oslo reported to Copenhagen that "the Jewish issue has yet to be officially addressed in Norway."[91] The Consul, however, reported rumors that the Norwegian Ministry of Justice was considering a regulation banning Jews from all public service and that the Ministry of Church Affairs had allegedly proposed to the Bishop a ban on marriages between Jews and non-Jews.

In October 1941, the Norwegian Ministry of Justice ordered all property owned by Jews to be registered. Non-compliance was punishable by death. The registration was accomplished by the Norwegian Office of Statistics, without any pressure from the Germans.[92] The Norwegian police used these registration lists in October 1942 when the Norwegian puppet government passed a law confiscating Jewish property.[93] Also in the autumn of 1941, Jews were prohibited from owning land and excluded from the civil service and the legal profession.[94]

Step by step, Norwegian Jews were deprived of their rights and their status as citizens. On January 20, 1942, the Norwegian Ministry of Police issued an order requiring all Jews to go to their local police headquarters to have their identification cards, border resident passes, permits, and employment cards stamped with a large letter "J". The order defined a Jew as (1) anyone with three full Jewish grandparents; (2) any Jewish bastard with two Jewish grandparents, if that person is a member of a Jewish congregation or marries a Jew; and (3) any member of a Jewish congregation.[95]

At the same time, Jews were required to register with the police and to report a great deal of personal information on a questionnaire, which included the identity of family members, membership in religious organizations, occupation, assets, and date of arrival in Norway. This information, which had to be continuously updated, was given to the Norwegian Security Police and the NS Party's statistical office.[96] These records were used in October and November 1942, when the Norwegian police arrested the Jews.

On February 1, 1942, Vidkun Quisling was appointed "minister president" of a puppet Nazi government. Quisling's NS (i.e., Nazi) party was the only political party the Germans permitted. Six weeks later, on March 12, 1942, Quisling reinstated Article 2 of Norway's constitution, which had been repealed in 1851, excluding Jews from the country and in effect turning Norwegian Jews, including those born in Norway, into aliens.

The climax of the attack on the Norwegian Jews came in the autumn of 1942. On October 26, the Norwegian State Police arrested all Jewish men over the age of sixteen, including the aged and sick, and placed them in concentration camps in Norway. The purported reason was the shooting on October 22 of a member of the Norwegian border police, a recent graduate of the Norwegian Nazi police academy, by a Norwegian fireman leading a group of Jews to the Swedish border. The fireman was court martialled and executed, along with one of the Jews attempting to escape. The others were sent to concentration camps and eventually deported to Nazi death camps. However, the shooting of the Norwegian policeman was simply the occasion for the round-up and deportation of the Norwegian Jews; there can be no doubt that it would have soon happened even if the shooting had not occurred.

The Norwegian police were extraordinarily diligent in making the arrests. If a person they were seeking was not at the address which he had listed when required to register earlier in the year, the police returned to his home later – sometimes several times the same day or on following days. If the person still could not be found, further efforts were made. Although some policemen and others who knew about the impending arrests warned Jews in advance, many who were warned stayed in their homes instead of leaving, perhaps because they did not know of any practical way to escape or because they knew that if caught they would almost certainly be summarily executed. Women and children were not arrested on October 26, but all women were required to report daily to the nearest police station.[97]

On the same day as the arrests of the male Norwegian Jews, the Quisling government enacted a law confiscating the property of all Norwegian and stateless Jews, and their spouses and minor children, for the benefit of the State Treasury. All gold and silver objects, as well as watches, were to go to the German security police as "a contribution to the war effort."[98] Creditors of the Jews were given one month (two months in the case of foreign creditors) to file claims against the assets.[99] On November 17, all Jews still at liberty (mainly women and children) were required to register with the local authorities, and copies of their registrations were sent to the Ministry of the Interior.[100]

On November 26, the Norwegian police arrested those who had not been included in the earlier round-up: Jewish women, children under the age of sixteen, the sick, the mentally ill, and the retarded. The November 26 operation was carefully planned, based on written instructions from K.A. Marthinsen, head of the Norwegian State Police.[101]

Between 9:00 p.m. and midnight on November 25, air raid sirens went off repeatedly to keep people off the streets. The arrests began at 5:00 a.m. the following morning. The Norwegian police went from house to house, using the addresses on registration lists the Jews had previously been required to fill out.

Inspector Knut Røed, the Norwegian State Police officer responsible for Oslo and eastern Norway, was in charge of arresting the Jews and turning them over to the Germans. Three hundred Norwegian policemen made the arrests. One hundred taxis and buses were requisitioned to take the victims to the pier of the Norwegian-American line at the Oslo port, where the German prison ship, *S.S. Donau,* was waiting for them. The way it worked was as follows: three police officers would take a taxi to the home of a Jewish family. If the taxi could not hold the entire family, one of the police officers would remain in the home with the persons who had not yet been transported, and the taxi would then return to pick up the remaining family members. Then the house or apartment would be sealed until a representative of the Norwegian Liquidation Board for Confiscated Jewish Property arrived to make an inventory of the family's property. As in the arrests of Jewish men a month earlier, the police diligently traced a victim's new address where an address was inaccurate because the person had moved.[102]

Neither the German occupation forces nor the Hirden (the Norwegian branch of the German Security Police) played any part in the arrests of the Jews or the confiscation of their property.[103] It was done by the Norwegian State Police and by government bureaucrats, who acted promptly and with alacrity. The Germans expected that the

Norwegian police would "act as the velvet glove for the occupiers' iron fist," and the Norwegians more than fulfilled their expectations of cooperation.[104] From the Germans' point of view, it was a great advantage for the Jews to be arrested by the local Norwegian police, who were familiar with the people in their own precincts. Besides, it was much easier for the Germans to let the Norwegians do their dirty work for them.[105]

Although the Norwegian bureaucracy was under general German control, its anti-Jewish actions were taken without coercion from German occupation authorities. Nor did the Norwegian public oppose these measures. There was a deep-seated feeling among a large part of the population that the Jews, however long they had lived in Norway, were a foreign element. An exhibit at the Museum of the Resistance in Oslo states that "Norwegian Nazis played an active part in baiting and persecuting Jews." While this statement is literally true, it is deeply misleading. Actions against the Jews were carried out by the "well-mannered regular Norwegian police," many of whom, however, had joined Quisling's NS party, as well as by other Norwegian career bureaucrats.[106]

For a country of three million people, only about two thousand of whom were Jews, Norway had an abundance of concentration camps, run entirely by Norwegians, not Germans. While not all prisoners in these camps were Jews, the Jewish inmates received particularly harsh treatment. The Falstad camp, near Trondheim in central Norway, has been described as "the worst prison camp in Norway and in some ways worse than Auschwitz."[107] At Falstad, people were beaten regularly, elderly and sick people were forced to crawl around a courtyard picking up fallen leaves with their mouths, and very hot water was poured over naked prisoners.[108]

There were three concentration camps in the vicinity of Oslo: Grini, Berg, and Bredtvedt. About half the prisoners were confined at Grini, the largest camp. Five Jewish women who were sent to Grini lived for several months in the basement, next to a room where prisoners were interrogated and tortured. Because of the shrieks, it was impossible for them to sleep.[109] Jews living in the Oslo area, including Johanna's nephew Hans Salomon, were imprisoned in the Berg concentration camp near Tønsberg, a town on the western shore of Oslo Fjord. The Berg camp in October 1942 was "totally unfit for human habitation, lacking water and toilet facilities."[110] Conditions at Berg were so atrocious that even the camp commander protested the transfer of more prisoners to the camp.[111]

Bredtvedt, where Johanna Salomon was imprisoned for three months, was used principally to hold prisoners destined for deportation to German death camps. Bredvedt was not as bad as some of the other Norwegian concentration camps.[112] Max Salomon, in exile in Sweden, wrote to his sister Gerda in the United States after Johanna's arrest in December 1942: "The only consolation is that Bredtvedt is said to be the most humane of these places, they are not treated as brutally as in the places run by the Gestapo." Nevertheless, Jewish prisoners received especially harsh treatment at Bredtvedt. The men were set to work digging ditches, while the women washed the floors, washed clothes, peeled potatoes, and did other menial work. Because the regular prison doctor (who was Quisling's personal physician) refused to treat Jews, the only doctors were Jewish prisoners, who of course had no medical supplies or instruments. The guards were young Norwegian Nazis who enjoyed playing at being SS men.[113] There also were concentration camps in Bergen on the west coast of Norway, Kristiansand in the south, and Tromsø in the far north.[114]

The arrest and deportation of the Norwegian Jews set off protests by Norwegian clergymen and educators. In a pastoral letter to clergymen, bishops tried to arouse public opinion against the arrests, denouncing anti-Semitism as unethical and contrary to the teachings of Christianity.[115] A number of bishops petitioned Quisling to intervene to save the Jews who had been arrested in October, and the petition was read from pulpits in several churches.[116] Quisling rejected the petition, declaring the Jews "an internationally destructive element."[117] He gave public expression to his virulent views in a speech in Trondheim in December 1942. There he said that the argument that a Jew cannot help being a Jew was an erroneous, even meaningless argument. If there is anything for which a person can be held responsible, he argued, it is certainly for being who he is. The Jew is not a Norwegian; he hails from the Orient and does not belong in Europe. He has no business being in Norway. Many Norwegians have married Jews, said Quisling, and their children are half Jews, which means real Jews, since the Jewish traits are so dominant. He went on to say that the only possible solution to the problem would be for the Jews to leave Europe for another region, preferably an island.[118]

Max reported to Gerda and Grete from Sweden on December 13, 1942 (the day before Johanna was arrested), that "the people of Norway are reacting violently" to the arrests; but the reports he relied on were incorrect. The attitude of the local population "ranged from active sympathy to apathy, indifference, and direct hostility leading to betrayal of Jews in hiding or to direct participation in their destruction."[119] In the regions of the country where there were no Jews, the arrests made no impression on the population. People in Norway could lead a fairly normal life during the occupation if they refrained from active resistance.[120] Norwegians who had Jewish neighbors did not protest their arrest or the theft of their property. There were no demonstrations against the actions of the Norwegian police, nor did the policemen or other Norwegians who assisted in the deportations refuse to obey orders.[121]

Ragnar Areklett, a Christian Norwegian who was living in the coastal town of Kristiansund at the time of the deportation of a six-year-old friend and neighbor, along with the boy's mother (his father and older brother had been arrested a month earlier), recalls that one thousand inhabitants of the town went to the pier to bid them goodbye, but nobody tried to interfere with their arrest and deportation.[122] Nobody can tell what would have happened if the Kristiansund townspeople had refused to give up the small boy and his mother; the point is that it was not tried. In contrast to the Danish population, the Norwegians made no attempt to prevent the deportation of the Jews. The German occupation authorities noted with satisfaction that there were no large-scale demonstrations of sympathy with the arrested Jews.[123] One SS officer in Norway opined in December 1942 that the Norwegians were egoists and would soon forget the actions taken against the Jews. This cynical prediction proved to be essentially correct.[124]

There was an organized Norwegian resistance movement, which helped to save about 800 Norwegian Jews. Members of this underground organization risked their own lives by hiding Jews, providing them with food and shelter in the sparsely populated districts of eastern Norway until guides who were familiar with the heavily forested, often snow-covered mountainous terrain could lead them past the German border patrols to safety in Sweden.[125] Many members of the resistance had gained their experience as members of Nansen Aid, a humanitarian organization named after the polar explorer Fridtjof Nansen, which saved the lives of many refugees from Soviet Russia during the 1920s.[126] In January 1943, Max wrote: "Actually everything was wonderfully organized and even people as old as 84 were carted to within half an hour's walk of the frontier."

One should not, however, overestimate the role of the Norwegian resistance. Fewer than 1,500 of its members died during the five years of the occupation, and only 162 of these as a result of direct clashes with the Germans.[127] There were others who acted clandestinely; for example, some Norwegian policemen, while ostensibly obeying the orders of their superiors, saved Jews by warning them of their impending arrests. However, the leaders of the Norwegian police, who had kept in close contact with the German police since the early 1930s, and the Norwegian civil service cooperated with the Germans and were even eager to assist the anti-Jewish actions.[128]

It should also be noted that saving Jews was not the prime concern of the Norwegian resistance, whose principal aims were to commit acts of sabotage and to assist in the escape to Sweden of young men, many of whom intended to find their way to England to join the Allied armed forces.[129] Max Salomon, living in Sweden in October 1942, wrote:

There has been quite an invasion of young men from Norway who came over the border in order to escape being drafted for slave work. Last month there came about 1,500 and I have had a chat with several of them. They are mostly country lads and they do not look undernourished, but they tell us it is very bad at Oslo and other towns.

In December 1942, a time of extreme jeopardy for Norwegian Jews who had thus far escaped arrest and deportation, the legation in Stockholm of the Norwegian government-in-exile based in London sent word informally to the Norwegian resistance that they should not help any more Jews escape to Sweden. The principal motive for the instruction was not so much anti-Semitism as fear that efforts to rescue old persons, women, and children might endanger the escape routes across the border. However, anti-Semitism was not unknown among the members of the resistance or among the Christian Norwegians they helped to escape.

Although the number of Norwegian Jews who died in German death camps was small compared to the catastrophic annihilation of the Jewish populations in Germany and most other German-occupied countries, the percentage of Norwegian Jews who died was high — higher than it was in many other European countries. In 1941-42, the Jewish population of Norway consisted of 2,173 individuals living in about 1,000 households. Of these, 1,536 Jews were registered with the Norwegian Ministry of Police as a result of the requirement imposed in January 1942.[130] The remainder, like Johanna's children

Max and Gerda, had fled the country in 1940 or gone into hiding. About 800 managed to escape to Sweden, many with the help of the Norwegian resistance movement, while 767 were deported to concentration camps. Only thirty of the deportees survived.[131] Thus, 48 percent of those who obeyed the registration order and 34 percent of the entire 1940 Jewish population of Norway were killed. By comparison, 26 percent of the French Jews and 14 percent of the Italian Jews died in the Holocaust.[132]

Several members of the Salomon family were living in Norway at the time of the German invasion. These were Johanna Salomon; her son, Max Salomon, and his wife and infant daughter; Johanna's daughter, Gerda Weill, and her five-year-old daughter; Johanna's nephew, Hans Salomon, and his wife, who was non-Jewish, and their two children; and Johanna's niece, Elly Salomon. Max and Gerda and their families escaped to Sweden in 1940; so only Johanna, Hans, and Elly were in Norway when the arrests and deportations occurred in late 1942. Johanna and Hans were able to escape from Norway in early 1943, but Elly died in the Holocaust.

Johanna Salomon with her daughter Grete.

Johanna
in Occupied Norway

$\longrightarrow\!\!\!\bullet$

{1940-1942}

WHEN THE GERMANS INVADED, Johanna Salomon, then sixty-nine, was living by herself in Voksenlia, a village outside Oslo. Believing, as did many other Norwegians, that the war would be over in a year or less and that somehow things would return to normal, she decided not to try to escape from Norway.[133] Her decision was also influenced by a pro-German Norwegian lawyer friend and neighbor, Sverre Helliksen, who advised her that the Germans would do her no harm. After the war, Helliksen was arrested, charged with treason as a Nazi collaborator, and held in prison for several months, although it is not clear whether he was ever tried or convicted.

Johanna's unperturbed attitude was by no means unusual; only about 150 of the 2,100 Jews living in Norway left the country in 1940. Johanna's children Max and Gerda, who escaped immediately after the German invasion, were exceptions. The suddenness of the invasion deprived many of the opportunity to escape. Flight entailed serious and unknown perils, including possible arrest and punishment if the attempt was unsuccessful. Some were held back by fear of reprisals against relatives who remained in Norway. Many elderly people, including Johanna, did not feel that they were up to the physical strain and emotional stress of an escape through the mountains to Sweden, at a time of year when the countryside still was snow covered.[134] Johanna mistakenly believed that her age would protect her from mistreatment at the hands of the Nazis.[135]

Other reasons kept Norwegian Jews in Norway. Sweden was the only practically accessible place of refuge, but in 1940 there was widespread expectation that sooner or later Sweden, too, would be invaded by the Germans. To some, it seemed safer to remain in one's native land than to be a refugee in a foreign country. Nor was it clear that Sweden, whose policy at the time was pro-German and anti-refugee, would accept Jews fleeing from Norway. As we will see, Swedish border officials did turn some of them back.

For other Norwegian Jews, force of habit, love of familiar surroundings, and bonds of friendship combined to create inertia: a feeling that perhaps it would be best to stay and hope that things would work out for the best. Finally, in 1940 German persecution of the Jews had not yet become the Holocaust; many did not anticipate that the Germans would attempt to destroy the Jewish population of Norway. In fact, on September 25, 1940, about six months after the German invasion, Reischskommisar Terboven promised amnesty to Norwegians who had fled Norway,[136] and he promised protection to all religious denominations. Some of the Jews who had fled in 1940 actually returned to Norway, believing that Terboven's assurance included them. This, of course, was a serious mistake. Many of those who returned were arrested and deported to Auschwitz in 1942 and 1943.[137]

Johanna steadfastly refused to consider fleeing to Sweden herself, even assuming that it was still possible to do so. Her letters to Gerda, who lived in Sweden during the first six months of the occupation of Norway, give no sense that she felt she was in any danger. In July 1940, she wrote: "Don't try talking me into coming over there; I don't like traveling that far. My foot easily gets tired, too, and then it starts hurting. As long as I rest frequently and don't stand on my feet for too long, it is okay. Don't worry about me." She even commiserated that Gerda and her five-year-old daughter, Dorrit, were alone in Sweden rather than with her in Norway. In June 1940 she wrote: "I am sitting here thinking only of you, how you are spending your Sundays alone in a strange city without any friends. Poor you and Dodo [this was Dorrit's nickname]."

For Johanna, the first two and a half years of the occupation were a time of increasing loneliness and privation, although she was not imprisoned or harmed. In 1940, when the Nazis, in their first overt act against the Jews, confiscated their radios, Johanna wrote to Gerda: "All radios are confiscated here, which is sad, as I really enjoyed the entertainment and music." None of her children or grandchildren remained in Norway. She spent much of her time knitting clothes and making jam and preserves, but she stopped making jam because she found that it was no fun making it only for herself.

In 1941, Johanna moved into the house at Furubråtveien 13 in Nordstrand that Max and Nora had abandoned when they fled to Sweden. Max and Nora's housekeeper, Hellbjørg Gjørvad, had remained in the house after the German invasion, but she took the precaution of burying the family's silverware under the gravel in the driveway. Although later in the war German officers requisitioned the house for their own use, they never found the silver, and Max and Nora dug it out of its hiding place after they returned in 1945.

For some time, Johanna shared the house with a tenant (an accountant named Sverre Sem) as well as with Hellbjørg, but Johanna did not get along well with Hellbjørg. In fact, her letters indicate that there were very few people with whom she did get along well.

Food and fuel became increasingly scarce. Firewood was the only fuel available, and it was rationed, as was electricity. Because of the shortage of fuel, Johanna could keep only one room in the house heated. With gasoline unobtainable, the streets were quiet and empty. As early as June 1940, Johanna wrote to Gerda: "You can only see people on bikes and all kinds of horse carriages coming out of their hiding places." She preferred to look at the brighter side of the situation (at least in letters to her daughter): "Our street has become delightfully calm now, . . . so we are no longer woken up in the morning by the noise of motors."

Because the German occupation cut off Norway's trade with the rest of the world, the country was dependent on Germany for most of its supplies. And Germany imposed a hard bargain, taking a maximum quantity of Norwegian exports, principally fish and metal products, in exchange for a minimum amount of wheat, fats, fodder, petroleum, and other essentials.[138] Mountainous, seabound Norway, only a small proportion of which was arable land, could not feed itself; food and other essentials were in short supply.

Johanna wrote to Gerda in March 1941: "Naturally, having guests over is difficult now; you always have to bring something along if you are to spend the whole day. When I got some ground meat last Sunday, the butcher told me that I wouldn't be able to get any more meat for another three weeks, and I heard other people say the same thing. Eggs are hard to get hold of, too, but we have plenty of fish, so we are not starving."

Johanna's son Harald was able to help her by sending packages from Copenhagen, where food was plentiful despite the occupation, including sausages, smoked pork, cheese, and even eggs. Unfortunately, only ten of the forty eggs he sent in one package arrived unbroken. Even her eldest son Max, who was living extremely frugally in rural Sweden, was able to send her food packages. In October 1941, Johanna reported to Gerda that 600 packages from private individuals were arriving monthly in Oslo as gifts. A doctor's order was needed in order to buy milk. But fruit and berries were available to pick and preserve. Life was dreary and unpleasant, but nobody starved.

Johanna wrote frequently to Gerda in Sweden until October 1940, when Gerda left for the United States. She continued to write to Gerda in the United States until December 1941, when the entry of the United States into war against Germany ended all contact between Norway and the U.S. Her letters were devoid of self-pity. She reported the details of her uneventful life, and she never ceased advising Gerda on how best to bring up her daughter. Considering her own straitened and increasingly perilous situation, Johanna's attempts to manage her daughter and granddaughter's lives by long distance may sound ludicrous, but Johanna could not shake her lifelong habit of trying to control the lives of her children. Perhaps, too, her continued involvement in the lives of her daughter and granddaughter took her mind off her own bleak situation. In October 1940, she wrote to Gerda and Dorrit, who were still living in Sweden: "I see that there have been some cases of poisoned drinking water in Sweden and that some people have died, so I hope you are boiling all your water. Moreover, there is a skin epidemic, so please be careful."

In February 1941, as the Nazi noose continued to

tighten around her own neck, this indomitable grand-mother wrote to Gerda in New York, where she was expected soon to arrive: "For quite some time now, [Dorrit] has only been around adults, but that is not good for a child! Get her into a school as quickly as possible, she enjoys other children, and they are the most suitable company for her. — And I would like to ask you to give her cod liver oil; everybody is taking it over here now; it is obligatory for all manual workers and school children, and the rest of us take it, too, and Dorrit has to drink it, as she needs something fortifying after the long journey."

And in August 1941, after Gerda and Dorrit had arrived in New York, Johanna, who had never in her life visited the United States, even advised Gerda about the perils of the New York climate: "Now winter is around the corner, and it can get very cold in New York. Wouldn't it be a good idea to have heavy winter coats made for yourself and Dorrit soon?"

After Germany went to war with the United States in December 1941, Johanna could no longer write to Gerda, but she kept in touch with Max in Sweden and with Harald in Denmark. In the summer or early autumn of 1942, Johanna moved out of the house in Nordstrand and became a patient at Vikersund Bad, for a health cure, but also because it had become too difficult for her to find enough food for herself at home. Vikersund Bad was a beautiful old spa situated on a lake near Oslo, with natural springs, mud baths, and a medical staff.

Meanwhile, as the German and Norwegian authorities prepared to arrest and deport the Norwegian Jews, Max and his wife Nora tried to persuade Johanna to try to join Harald in Denmark, where Jews were safe from German persecution, at least for the time being. They also implored

Harald to do everything he could to get Johanna out of Norway. Nothing came of these efforts.

Johanna escaped arrest (and deportation) on November 26, 1942, when the Norwegian police arrested Jewish women and children, because she was not living at the home address shown on her registration with the police, but was staying at Vikersund Bad. Thus, the police did not immediately find her. However, they searched diligently for Jews who had slipped their net and, on December 14, Johanna was arrested at the old spa and imprisoned in the Bredtvedt concentration camp at Grorud, on the outskirts of Oslo.[139] Under the anti-Semitic law adopted by the Norwegian government on October 26, 1942, all her property was confiscated.[140] In fact, the arresting police stole all of the personal possessions that she had with her when she was arrested, including her clothes and eyeglasses. At Bredtvedt, she was able to get in touch with Gjørvad, who brought some underwear and stockings to her at the prison.

Bredtvedt was essentially a holding camp the Norwegian police used to detain Jews and others arrested in northern Norway and brought there while they waited for a ship in which to deport them. Although Bredtvedt was not the worst Norwegian concentration camp it was a terrible place, especially for a seventy-one-year-old woman not in good health. When she was arrested and taken there, she must have known that eighteen days earlier the German prison ship *S.S. Donau* had sailed from Oslo with over 500 Jews, many of them taken from Bredtvedt, destined for Auschwitz. By December 1942, it was generally known throughout Europe that no Jews returned from deportation. Fear cannot have been far from her thoughts at any time during her imprisonment.

Bredtvedt Prison, Oslo, where Johanna was imprisoned in 1942–43.

The Rescue of Johanna

———

{1942-1943}

SHEER GOOD LUCK played a large part in saving Johanna from deportation to Auschwitz. If she had been in her home when the Norwegian State Police attempted to arrest every Jew still living in freedom in Norway, including women and children of all ages, she would have certainly have been deported. Like her niece Elly Salomon, Johanna would have been taken directly to the German prison ship *Donau,* which sailed Germany the same afternoon. When she finally was arrested on December 14, Johanna was imprisoned at Bredtvedt to await the arrival of another prison ship.[141] The delay gave Johanna precious time during which a miracle might save her.

It could be said that a miracle did occur, not because of divine intervention but because the Danish consul-general in Oslo, Hans Henning Schrøder, and his superiors at the Danish Ministry of Foreign Affairs (MFA) in Copenhagen went to extraordinary lengths to obtain Johanna's release from prison and to remove her to the comparative safety of Denmark.

In 1942, Schrøder was forty-eight. His educational background was in the law, but he had been a career officer of the MFA since 1916. He came from a distinguished Danish family, his father having been director of the National Treasury. Before taking up the post of consul-general in Oslo in 1940, he had served his government in New York, Washington, D.C., Beijing, Leningrad, and Stockholm. He had also been the legation secretary in Oslo in 1930, so he was no stranger to the country; upon his arrival as the newly appointed consul-general, he told Norwegian newspaper reporters that he had always longed to return there. "My work will mainly consist of handling regular consular business, assisting Danes who are in this country, and promoting trade relations," he said in a typically matter-of-fact Danish way. He also told the reporters that he planned to do some skiing while in Norway. In view of the cataclysmic events that followed, it is unlikely that he did much skiing during his Norwegian tour of duty.[142]

Schrøder was posted to Oslo shortly before the German invasion. Although Denmark also was occupied by Germany, unlike Norway, during the first three years of the occupation it maintained its formal status as an independent, neutral nation with its own elected government. The MFA continued to be in charge of the Danish consular service, subject to German control of some matters, including the granting of visas for entry into the country.

As Schrøder had told the Norwegian newspapers, one of his main tasks as consul-general was to protect the interests of Danish citizens living in Norway. A small number of these people were Jewish. According to a list compiled by Schrøder, they included Johanna, her nephew Hans Salomon, Hans's wife Gunvor (who was not Jewish) and their two children, and Johanna's niece Elly Salomon. From the point of view of the Danish government, a Danish citizen of Jewish origin was entitled to the same protection as any other Dane. Thus, the Danish government, unlike those of other occupied countries, refused to cooperate with the Germans in taking the first step in the process that led to their death in the Holocaust: stripping the Jews of their rights and status as citizens of their country.

In 1942, as the vise tightened around the Norwegian Jews, anxiety also spread among Danish Jews living in Norway. Their anxiety intensified to alarm on October 26 when the Norwegian police began to arrest and imprison Norwegian Jewish men and to confiscate Jewish assets, and that alarm intensified still further when, on November 17, the Norwegian government passed another law requiring all Jews residing in Norway to register with the local police.

The German order for the arrest of Norwegian Jews specified that Danish Jews should not be arrested. At the time, there were about a dozen Danish Jews living in Norway.[143] Several Danish Jews went to their consulate in Oslo for advice and guidance as to whether the registration requirement applied to them.[144] Schrøder consulted an official of the Norwegian Ministry of the Interior, who stated that only those persons who knew or had a solid reason to believe they had at least a quarter of Jewish blood were required to register. This of course provided no reassurance to the Danish Jews that they were safe. Nor did the Norwegian official give Schrøder any assurance that the Danish Jews would not be deported along with Norwegian Jews. Furthermore, the Germans refused to issue visas to Danish Jews to enable them to return to Denmark where, at least for the time being, the Danish government protected Jews from German persecution.

In early November, the German authorities in Denmark

denied entry visas to three Danish Jews who were living in Norway: Ivar and Amalie Nathanson and Martha Kirschner. On November 7, as soon as the officials at the Danish Ministry of Justice learned of the German action, they reminded their colleagues at the MFA that in earlier negotiations between the Danish and German authorities the Germans had reassured the Danes that Danish citizens would not be denied permission to reenter Denmark from abroad except on very strong grounds, and that any such denial would not be based on the individual's race.[145]

At this point, the MFA intervened with the German authorities in Copenhagen on the question of the entry visas. It is remarkable that, in the winter of 1942-43, senior government officials of German-occupied Denmark were willing to go to great lengths to save a handful of their Jewish citizens who were living abroad. Furthermore, the MFA acted very quickly, because it regarded the matter as urgent. The Danish officials knew that Danish Jews living in Norway were in peril of being arrested and deported to Auschwitz if they were denied permission to return to Denmark.

On November 11, 1942, Nils Svenningsen, director general of the MFA and its highest official below Cabinet rank, met with a Dr. Stalmann of the German legation in Copenhagen and asked him whether Jews seeking entry visas to Denmark would be treated differently from other Danish citizens. Svenningsen stated that it was the MFA's position that no Danish citizen, Jewish or non-Jewish, could be denied entry into the country. Stalmann reassured Svenningsen that, in accord with rules agreed upon between the two countries in November 1940, no distinctions would be made on the basis of race. Under these rules,

Danes who wished to leave or enter the country were required to apply to the Danish authorities, who would make a recommendation to the Germans on each application. Thus, a Dane living in Norway needed a visa to enter Denmark, and the Germans controlled the issuance of the visas. When the rules were adopted, the Germans had assured the Danes that their enforcement would not be harsh and that Jewish Danes would not be targeted.

By late 1942, however, the deportation and murder of European Jews was in full swing, and German occupation authorities in Denmark were no longer willing to honor the assurances they had made to the Danish government in 1940. They still refused to issue entry visas to Danish Jews living in Norway. To some extent, the hardening of the Germans' attitude may have been the result of concessions made by the MFA to the German occupiers. When the visa rules were first adopted, the form an applicant filled out required no information about his or her race or religion. After later negotiations, the Danes agreed to amend the form, effective July 1942, to include questions about the applicant's race (but not about the race of the applicant's parents and grandparents).

Nevertheless, the MFA continued to press the Germans to approve the issuance of entry visas to the Danish Jews in Norway. This was largely the work of a Danish MFA official named H.J. Hansen, who, like Schrøder, was an experienced career officer. His father came from a prominent landowning family in Zealand (the island on which Copenhagen is situated) and had served as a member of the King's Council in the late nineteenth century. H.J. Hansen was educated as a political scientist and joined the MFA in 1920. Between the wars, he served at Danish consulates in

Chicago, Seattle, and various European cities. In 1939, at the age of fifty, he was promoted to the position of section chief of the MFA in Copenhagen.

On November 13, 1942, Hansen brought up the matter of entry visas for Danish Jews living in Norway with Franz Machowetz, the secretary of the German legation in Copenhagen, who was also head of the legation's passport office. In response, Machowetz expressed concern that if the Danish Jews were permitted to leave Norway they might disappear in transit, since they would be traveling by train through neutral Sweden on their way from Oslo to Copenhagen. Hansen answered that the fear seemed unfounded because they could be guarded while en route. He also pointed out that the three Danish Jews whose entry visas had been denied had already obtained exit visas from the German passport authorities in Norway. Machowetz promised Hansen that he would evaluate the case.[146]

Ten days later, however, Schrøder reported to the MFA from Oslo that the Norwegian exit visas of the Nathansohns and Mrs. Kirschner had been rescinded, presumably at the request of the German legation in Denmark. In an internal memorandum, Hansen, the MFA section chief, noted that the Germans' fear that the Jews might disappear in Sweden while in transit could be assuaged by providing proper escort for them.

On November 28, Mrs. Kirschner's brother, who was living in Denmark, asked the MFA to find out if she was still in Norway. He had heard over the Swedish radio about the deportation of Norwegian Jews to Poland, and he feared that his sister might have been one of those deported. Although Schrøder was able to confirm that the

Nathansohns and another Danish-Jewish couple, Marcus and Regine Wulff, were still in Norway (the Wulffs were imprisoned with Johanna Salomon at Bredtvedt), he was unable to obtain any information about Mrs. Kirschner. The Norwegian police told him that she had not been arrested, but Schrøder was unable to get in touch with her at her home or anywhere else. It is not clear whether or not Mrs. Kirschner had been deported; but it is worth noting that Johanna's niece, Elly Salomon, had likewise disappeared, and Schrøder and the MFA continued to assume, for more than a month after she was deported on November 26, that she was alive in Norway.

The situation of the Danish Jews living in Norway remained unclear. On December 3, the MFA asked Schrøder to inform the authorities in Norway that the Danish government assumed that Danish Jews would not be affected by the measures taken against the Norwegian Jews. Having ascertained that Swedish Jews living in Norway would not be affected by the Norwegian anti-Jewish laws, Schrøder told the German authorities that he assumed the same applied to the very small number of Danish Jews. The Germans said that there was a difference between neutral Sweden and the countries occupied by Germany, to which Schrøder defiantly replied that Denmark was an independent country and did not fall into the same category as the other occupied countries. Although Schrøder still believed from his discussions with the German and Norwegian authorities that the Danish Jews would not be deported, he urged the MFA to speed the processing of their applications for entry visas to Denmark. The MFA replied that the applications had been submitted to the German legation in Copenhagen and that the MFA was staying in contact with the Germans "to hasten the processing of the case and to push for a positive answer."[147]

Thus, in Copenhagen as well as in Oslo, representatives of the Danish government continued to make every possible effort to repatriate Danish Jews living in Norway. On December 12 (two days before Johanna Salomon's arrest), Hansen, the MFA section chief, again discussed with Machowetz, the German legation secretary, the question of entry visas for Danish Jews in Norway who wished to return to Denmark. Machowetz said that he was unable to give a positive answer on this subject. Hansen asked him whether concern that the Jews might disappear in transit through Sweden was at the root of the problem. Machowetz replied, chillingly (in view of the fact that total destruction of European Jews was in full operation at this time), that "the question had to be viewed in the context of the Jewish issue as a whole."

Hansen's account of the meeting continues, expressing perfectly the attitude the Danish government took toward its Jewish citizens: "Moreover, he [Machowetz] opined that it could not be in Denmark's interest to receive any more Jews. I answered that the people in question were Danish citizens, after all, so the Danish authorities could not accept such a position."[148] One can only admire the decency, courage, and professionalism of this official, who was willing to stand up to the German occupiers of his country on behalf of a few of its Jewish citizens. As Hannah Arendt wrote two decades later, while some other countries, such as Bulgaria and Italy, resisted the German war of extermination against the Jews by subterfuge, "only the Danes dared speak out on the subject to their German masters."[149]

As for Machowetz's concern about the Jews' possible disappearance in transit through Sweden, Hansen replied that arrangements could be made for the journey to occur under proper escort. Again, Machowetz repeated his prediction (which could be regarded as a thinly veiled threat against all Danish Jews, including those living in Denmark) that the issue of reentry of Danish Jews abroad would be settled "in connection with an overall solution to the Danish Jewish issue," adding that "it would hardly be long before this must be addressed." Ignoring this last remark, Hansen ended the meeting by stating that the MFA reserved the right to readdress the issue of the entry visas if the Germans did not change their minds.

This is how matters stood on December 14, 1942, when Johanna Salomon was arrested at the spa of Vikersund Bad and locked up in the Bredtvedt prison camp. Furthermore, aside from the difficulty of obtaining a visa to enter Denmark, Johanna had an additional problem: it was by no means clear that she was a Danish citizen. In fact, she herself believed she was Norwegian and had so stated when she was required to fill out her "Questionnaire for Jews" with the Norwegian police in March 1942.

The question of Johanna's citizenship was a complicated one. Johanna was born in Poland, but her parents had acquired German citizenship when she was a child. Her deceased husband, Simon, was born in Denmark and was a Danish citizen when the couple married in 1896. Three years later, Simon was naturalized as a Norwegian citizen, and under Norwegian law a wife automatically acquired the citizenship of her husband. In 1915, however, Simon and Johanna returned to Denmark, where Simon died a year later. Under Norwegian law, a naturalized Norwegian citizen lost his citizenship by taking up residence in another country. He therefore regained his Danish citizenship, and Johanna likewise became a Danish citizen. To further complicate the matter, Johanna had returned to Norway in 1923 and had lived there continuously until the time of her arrest in 1942. Thus, any claim she might have of Danish citizenship rested on her having moved to Denmark with her husband in 1915. In fact, she had spent most of her adult life in Norway, her only home was in Norway, she carried a Norwegian passport, and she considered herself a citizen of Norway.

The chance of survival of an elderly Norwegian Jewish woman who was detained in a concentration camp in Norway in December 1942 was just about zero. She would almost certainly have been placed aboard the *S.S. Gotenland*, which carried 158 Jewish deportees from Norway in February 1943, and gassed immediately upon her arrival at Auschwitz, assuming that she survived the unspeakable ordeal of the journey, which meant being packed into a prison ship and then into a freight car for at least a day or two without food or water. Her only hope of survival seemed to lie in proving that she was a Danish citizen and therefore eligible for an entry visa into Denmark. But Johanna, imprisoned at Bredtvedt, did not understand that her life depended on establishing that her nationality was Danish.

On December 28, two weeks after her arrest, Johanna wrote a letter to Schrøder from Bredtvedt prison asking for his assistance in obtaining her release. She wrote that she wished to go to Denmark to stay with her son Harald, who had been a Danish citizen since 1927 and was employed as medalist at the Royal Danish Mint.[150] She made no claim of Danish citizenship but on the contrary insisted that she had been a Norwegian citizen since 1896 (in fact she had been naturalized in 1899). Like a number of other Norwegian Jews, she mistakenly thought she was safe because she was Norwegian.

Meanwhile, Harald Salomon had learned of his mother's arrest and had retained a prominent Copenhagen lawyer, H.H. Bruun, to help obtain her release. On January 4, 1943, Bruun wrote to Schrøder, whom he apparently knew socially (he ended his letter with the words "Please accept my friendly greetings to you and your wife, and I wish you a Happy New Year."). Bruun, like Johanna, seemed not to appreciate the vital importance of establishing that Johanna was a Danish citizen; his only request of Schrøder was that he provide documentation that Simon had been a *Norwegian* citizen.[151] Schrøder promptly passed on Bruun's request to the Norwegian Ministry of the Interior.[152]

At this point, Schrøder took it upon himself to try to help Johanna. He replied to her letter from prison, not too subtly suggesting to her that perhaps she was a Danish citizen after all. He wrote: "Before further undertakings are conducted, please let us know whether you are still a Norwegian citizen and permanently residing in Norway, or whether you maintained residence in Denmark for many years and hence obtained Danish nationality." Johanna, however, did not pick up the hint. She replied stubbornly on January 20: "I would like to inform you that I am still a Norwegian citizen and permanently residing [in Norway]."[153]

However, even if Johanna and her son's lawyer did not understand how vital it was to establish her Danish citizenship, Schrøder did, and it seemed he would do what he could to help her.

The MFA, perhaps at the prompting of Johanna's son Harald, also was bent on saving her, even if she could not (or would not) claim Danish citizenship. On January 21, the MFA sent a telegram to Schrøder, suggesting a different ground for her release: "The Consulate is . . . kindly requested to consider providing assistance to Mrs. Johanna Salomon, who presumably is a Norwegian citizen, considering her connection to Denmark and her advanced age." At this point, the Norwegian Nazi government inadvertently came to Johanna's rescue. Responding to Bruun's inquiry about Simon's citizenship that Schrøder had previously passed on to the Norwegian Ministry of the Interior, the Ministry notified Schrøder that, having looked into the matter, its Office of Constitutional Law concluded that Simon had lost his Norwegian citizenship by moving back to Denmark in 1914 (it was actually in 1915). Schrøder reported this to the MFA, adding that there was no information as to whether Johanna had regained her Norwegian citizenship during her twenty-year stay in the country beginning in 1923. At this point, Schrøder formally requested the commander of the German Security Police in Norway to release Johanna from prison.

While the issue of Johanna's citizenship was still in doubt, the situation of the Danish Jews living in Norway remained a matter of great concern not only to themselves but also to the Danish government. Schrøder continued to try to clarify their status, in the context of the ongoing Norwegian persecution of the Jews. In January 1943, he raised the question with a minister of the Norwegian government named Hagelin, who assured him that the Danish

Jews were in no danger. Schrøder's report to the MFA carries a strong suggestion that the Norwegian government's anti-Jewish measures were being taken without prompting from the Germans:

> Furthermore, [Hagelin] expressed regret regarding the unnecessarily brutal methods that had been used against the Jews as a whole, and said that the German authorities had indicated that the persecution of the Jews had now ended. (The German officials hinted that it was the Norwegian Government that took the initiative against the Jews, and that they were puzzled that the local Government went so much further than what had been the case in Germany.)

Even if one recognizes that the supposed puzzlement of the German officials was totally dishonest, given their intention to murder all the Jews of Europe, there can be no doubt that the Quisling government was sincere in its desire to destroy Norway's Jewish population. However, when Schrøder inquired of Norwegian officials about the status of the Danish Jews, they referred him to the German authorities. He therefore took the matter up with a Dr. Schiedermaier of the Reich Commissariat in Norway, who told him that it was probably safe to assume that Danish Jews in Norway would be treated in the same way as Swedish Jews; that is, their property would not be confiscated and they would not be deported.

Schrøder was not, however, persuaded by these reassurances. He reported to the MFA that President-Minister Vidkun Quisling, the head of the Norwegian puppet government, did not appear to share Hagelin's relatively moderate views. Schrøder referred to "some very aggressive statements against the Jews" and added : "After these statements, one has to assume that the Jewish issue has not been put to rest in Norway, after all. The consequence of Quisling's view must be that foreign Jews will be denied residence in Norway. . . ." [154]

In the winter of 1942-43, the German government had not yet decided to extend the Final Solution to the Danish Jews. Furthermore, the Germans did not wish to anger unduly the Danish government or to upset the collaborative arrangements that they had with it. The Germans were therefore not unresponsive to the pressure the Danish government was exerting on it to spare the Danish Jews living in Norway. In January 1943, SS Hauptsturmführer Wilhelm Wagner (the same man who had supervised the deportation of 532 Norwegian Jews two months earlier), whom Schrøder described as "one of the higher officials of the German Security Police," asked for a meeting with Schrøder and told him confidentially that Quisling wanted all foreign Jews to leave Norway. His clear implication was that any Danish Jews who remained in Norway would be deported. Wagner inquired about the possibility of obtaining entry visas for the Danish Jews, adding that the German passport office would issue exit visas from Norway to all Danish Jews. Schrøder asked Wagner to inform the German Embassy in Copenhagen that the SS wanted the entry visas to be granted.

Wagner then reviewed with Schrøder a list of nine Danish Jews who might be considered for the granting of entry visas to Denmark. Ironically, this list included not only Johanna and Hans Salomon and his wife and children, but also Elly Salomon, whom the Nazis had deported and killed over a month earlier. A few days later, however, Schrøder was informed by the German Security Police that Elly had reported herself as a Norwegian when she was arrested on November 26 and that she had been "evacuated."[155] By this time, Schrøder and other Danish officials were well aware that "evacuation" was a German euphemism for deportation to Poland and a death camp.

At this point, Johanna received support from an unexpected source. On January 16, 1943, Sverre Helliksen, Johanna's pro-Nazi friend who had advised her in April 1940 to remain in Norway rather than to flee, wrote to Håkon Høst, a Norwegian Nazi official who had been named trustee of her confiscated assets. Helliksen told Høst that Johanna had been sent to Bredtvedt by mistake, that she was seventy-two years of age, heartsick, with no relatives in Norway. It is doubtful whether Helliksen's letter had any impact on Johanna's case. There can be no doubt, however, that the determined persistence of the Danish government to save the Danish Jews in Norway was having an influence on both German and Norwegian authorities.

From then on, things moved swiftly. Knowing that Johanna was in danger of being deported, Schrøder wasted no time taking advantage of the Norwegian government's conclusion that Simon Salomon had ceased to be a Norwegian citizen when he left Norway in 1915, and that therefore his wife, Johanna, was a Danish citizen despite her protestations to the contrary. On January 26, Schrøder requested the Norwegian Ministry of Foreign Affairs to release Johanna. On the same day, he reported to the MFA in Copenhagen that the Norwegian Department of Interior Affairs was requesting information as to whether

Johanna had followed her husband to Denmark in 1914 (or 1915) and remained there until she returned to Norway in 1923. Acting with exceptionally unbureaucratic speed, the MFA replied in the affirmative on the very next day, telling Schrøder that Johanna should be considered a Danish citizen pursuant to the Danish law that a wife's citizenship followed the citizenship of her husband. On January 30, 1943, the Norwegian Ministry of the Interior requested the head of the Safety Police to release Johanna and the other Danish Jews from prison, and requested the Ministry of Finance to strike their names from the list of Jews whose assets had been confiscated, "as it has turned out that . . . they are Danish citizens."[156]

Despite these favorable developments, the issue of the Danish entry visas was still unresolved. Spurred by an urgent memorandum from Schrøder on February 5 that Danish Jews would no longer be allowed to live in Norway, Hansen, the MFA section chief, again raised the issue with the German legation in Copenhagen. This time, the Germans informed Hansen confidentially that entry visas would be issued to those who had already applied for them, as well as to Johanna once her application was received.[157] The decision to grant the entry visas may have been the result of a request made by Wagner, the SS man in Oslo whose aim now was to get the Danish Jews out of Norway, pursuant to Schrøder's earlier discussion with him. On February 10, the MFA was able to report to Schrøder that entry visas to Denmark could be expected to be granted for sixteen persons: Johanna, her nephew Hans and his wife Gunvor and their two children, and eleven others, including four minor children. All except Gunvor were Jewish or half-Jewish.[158]

Johanna was released from prison in late February or early March 1943. The Danish consul-general presented her with a Danish passport and entry visa on March 2, and she arrived in Denmark on March 11.[159] She traveled from Norway to Denmark with a few other Danish Jews by train through Sweden, perhaps guarded by Swedish or Danish officials to prevent escape into that country. The issuance of the passport did not, however, represent an acknowledgement by the Danish government that she was a Danish citizen. Soon after the war ended, when Johanna was living in Denmark, she told a friend that she was trying to retrieve her Norwegian passport and that the Danish passport she had received in 1943 was only a "travel passport," which didn't entitle her to Danish citizenship. She added that "at the time being, I myself don't even know what I am."

It seems likely that the MFA and Schrøder issued the passport to her in 1943 solely to obtain her release from Bredtvedt and repatriation to Denmark, irrespective of whether or not she could legitimately claim Danish citizenship. This conclusion is supported by the fact that in 1946 Johanna retrieved her Norwegian passport, even though by that time she was living permanently in Denmark.

While Johanna was at Bredtvedt, Norwegian officials had made a list of the possessions in her house, including a large suitcase containing clothes and linens which her daughter Gerda had left behind when she fled Norway in 1940, in order to begin confiscation proceedings pursuant to the government order of October 26, 1942. Once the order was rescinded with regard to Johanna, her property, including her bank accounts, was returned to her, minus a number of items that apparently were stolen.

Johanna was able to visit her wartime home in Nordstrand after her release from prison. "I lost my only diamond ring," she wrote to Gerda three years later, "and there was nobody but Gjørvad [her companion] and myself in the house. I desperately searched for it, but couldn't find it anywhere. Then the Germans scheduled my departure from Oslo, and I had to leave. I asked her several times, but she answered 'no,' she could not understand it."

However, before she left Norway Johanna managed to entrust Gerda's jewelry and a watch to Schrøder, and he returned these items to her after the end of the war. Johanna also had time to sell Gerda's furniture and a fur coat and to deposit the proceeds in a bank account in Oslo. In addition, she was able to take an extraordinary number of possessions with her in the train to Copenhagen in March 1943, including wicker furniture, a desk, a bed, carpets, paintings, silverware, and a fur coat (which she wore on the journey). She also was able to bring Gerda's suitcase and even Gerda's skis. After arriving in Denmark, Johanna wrote several letters to Høst, the Norwegian Nazi trustee, concerning her confiscated property that was still missing, including the clothes she had with her when she was arrested at Vikersund Bad, some gloves, a brooch, a clothing ration card, and 729.55 kroner in cash. After the war ended, her son Max continued to pursue the matter, and the cash was finally restored to her bank account in December 1947.

When Johanna arrived in Copenhagen, she went to stay with Harald and his family in Charlottenlund, a Copenhagen suburb. She did not get along with Else, Harald's wife, and she soon moved to a nearby old-age home which, she wrote to a friend in Norway in September

1943, "will be my home from now on." Twelve elderly people lived there; she was the youngest of them. She furnished her large spacious room with household items she had brought with her from Norway, including porch furniture, a writing desk, a settee, rugs, and curtains. "If only peace will come," she wrote, "I would be perfectly happy with my life." Two weeks after she wrote this, the German decision to arrest the Danish Jews forced her to go into hiding and flee to Sweden.

Schrøder remained consul-general in Oslo until June 1945, one month after the European war ended. Just before he left, he received this letter from a (probably non-Jewish) Dane who lived in Norway during the war:

> Please allow me, Mr. Consul General, to express in
> this way my gratitude for all the help you have given
> to my family and myself throughout the long and
> terrible years of war.
>
> Whenever I visited the Consulate to present my
> concerns to you, I always returned home in good
> hopes after our conversations.
> . . .
> Wishing you many good years ahead in the services of
> our beloved Denmark, I remain. . . . Wiggo
> Christensen.[160]

After the war, Schrøder served for a year as the Danish consul-general in New York, but there is no indication that the Jewish community in New York — or anyone else — was aware of the role he played in saving the Danish Jews in Norway. The *New York Times* mentioned his name only twice during his sojourn there, the first time announcing his appointment in 1946 and the second time reporting that the Scandinavian-American Women's Association had hosted a luncheon for him before his departure from New York in 1947.[161]

It is improbable that Schrøder would have sought acclaim or gratitude for his deeds. Most likely his view was that he was just doing his job: to protect the interests of Danish citizens. When he retired in 1962, he received numerous tributes for his long service with the MFA, but none specifically for his efforts on behalf of the Jewish Danes living in Norway under the German occupation. The only recognition for his wartime work came from the Red Cross, which honored him in 1947 for his role in distributing food packages in Norway. Similarly, Hansen's unyielding insistence to the German occupiers of Denmark that he had a duty to protect all Danish citizens, including those who were Jewish, apparently went unnoticed.

Perhaps one should not be surprised that no public accolades went to these two two career officers for their crucial (but perhaps to them routine) work of these on behalf of the Danish Jews. What is surprising is that neither Johanna nor any other member of the Salomon family seems to have understood or commented on the fact that Schrøder, Hansen, and the MFA saved her life. In the many letters she wrote to her daughter Gerda after her escape from Denmark to Sweden in October 1943, she did not once mention her earlier rescue from Norway, although she described in some detail the belongings that she either left in Norway or brought with her to Denmark. The omission seems strange, especially considering the fact that she had written to Schrøder from Bredtvedt prison in

December 1942 asking for his help in obtaining her release and repatriation to Denmark — help which was immediately forthcoming.

Harald believed that he was the instrument of his mother's escape from Norway. After he and his family and Johanna all arrived in Sweden in October 1943, he wrote to Gerda: "I managed to rescue Mother from the grip of the assassins once, but the second time was a close call." Perhaps his belief in his own influence on the outcome is understandable; he may have thought that his prominence and contacts in Denmark enabled his lawyer to pull some strings on Johanna's behalf. He may also have discussed his mother's plight with people whom he knew at the MFA, although the MFA's files do not contain a record of any such conversation. Furthermore, Harald's status as a prominent Danish citizen might have increased the willingness of the MFA to help Johanna even though she never claimed to be a Danish citizen. Nevertheless, it was largely due to the tireless efforts of Schrøder, Hansen, and other MFA officials in Copenhagen that Johanna was saved from being murdered at Auschwitz, along with other Jews in Norway who claimed to be Danish citizens but, unlike Johanna, did not have any influential family connections.

Victims of the Shoah in Norway

Name (Surname, First Name)	Salomon, Elly
Address	Theresesgt. 35 B, v. 407
City/Municipality	Oslo
Date of Birth	23.07.1910 Sex ☐M ☒F
Citizenship	Norwegian

Larger photo

Deported	☒Yes ☐No Auschwitz-number
Survived deportation	☐Yes ☒No
Died in Norway	☐Yes ☒No
Deportation ship	Donau November 26th 1942
Probable date of death	01.12.1942
Main Source	Confiscation lists
Comment	Born in Oslo, daughter of Siegmund Salomon, b. 1858 in Copenhagen, Denmark, d. 1943 in Copenhagen, and Melitta, née Rosenthal, b. 1878 in Lübeck, Germany. Commercial school, studies in England and France. Sister to Hans Salomon, b. 1901. He was not deported due to Danish citizenship.

Shoah documentation of Elly Salomon's death at Auschwitz.
(Courtesy of Bjarte Bruland.) *Below, memorial to the deportation of the Norwegian Jews, Oslo.* (Courtesy of Ragnar Areklett.)

The Murder of Elly

{1942}

ELLY SALOMON was not blessed with the luck of her aunt Johanna. She was in her Oslo apartment in the early morning hours of November 26, 1942, when she was arrested by the Norwegian police and taken to the prison ship *Donau* waiting in the Oslo port to leave for Germany. The *Donau* sailed for Auschwitz on the same day with over 500 other Norwegian Jews, giving the Danish authorities no opportunity to establish that she could claim Danish citizenship and thus be saved. Elly's deportation occurred with the willing if not zealous assistance and complicity of the Norwegian authorities.

Elly Salomon was the only member of the Salomon family in Scandinavia known to have died in the Holocaust. She was the fifth child, and only surviving daughter, of the six children of Siegmund and Melitta Salomon (an older daughter, Anny, had died at the age of sixteen). Elly was born in Oslo on July 26, 1910. Her family moved to Denmark about three years later when Siegmund retired from active management of the Salomon Shoe Factory. After studying in England and France, Elly returned to Norway in the 1930s to live with her brother

Hans and sister-in-law Gunvor in the Valdres valley, a rural area in southern Norway, about two and a half hours' travel from Oslo, where Hans was in the shoe business. Because she disliked the harsh climate of Valdres, she soon moved to Oslo, where she took a job as a secretary. Never married, Elly lived by herself in a one-room apartment. It seems that she was an amateur artist and craftswoman, because the detailed inventory of her possessions compiled by the Norwegian Confiscation Board after she was arrested included a paint box, a drawing board, and a handwork kit.

The police awakened Elly in the early morning without warning and shoved her into a taxi requisitioned for that purpose. According to the German Security Police, she told the arresting policemen that she was a Norwegian citizen; if she had claimed to be Danish, as she might plausibly have done, it is possible that she would not have been deported. Ironically, in January 1943 Hans Henning Schröder, the Danish consul-general in Oslo, listed Elly Salomon in a dispatch to the Danish Foreign Ministry in Copenhagen as one of the Danish Jews who might be considered for the granting of an entry visa to Denmark. Thus, nearly two months after Elly's death, neither Schröder nor members of Elly's family knew that she had already been deported and killed.

When she was arrested, Elly was not permitted to take any personal possessions except ration cards for four days. She was taken directly from her home to the pier where the German prison ship *S.S. Donau* lay waiting. On the pier, the Norwegian police behaved brutally, even to women, babies, the old, and the sick. It was here that the Norwegians handed the victims over to the German SS (i.e., security police) officers, under the command of Hauptsturmführer (i.e., Captain) Wilhelm Wagner, who may have been Adolf Eichmann's representative in Norway.[162] The dock area was crowded with police guards, Jews who had been arrested the same day in their homes or in hospitals, and Jews who had been brought from Norwegian concentration camps for deportation on the *Donau*. "According to eyewitness reports violent scenes took place at the quay in Oslo before the *Donau* left port. Nobody was allowed to assist the old and disabled. Women and children were hoisted on board in a cattlesling."[163]

The scene was unimaginable in its barbarity. The sick on stretchers were thrown on board. The Jews were terrorized and forced to carry heavy packages, including potato sacks, at an accelerated tempo. Families were separated amid cries of grief and despair. On board, they were stowed like cattle, the women and children in the bow, the men in the stern. Children clung to their parents in fright. Some of the young women on board, perhaps including Elly, volunteered to help as nannies for the children.[164]

On orders from Berlin, food for four days was provided on the ship. Shortly before the *Donau* sailed from Oslo at 3:00 p.m. on November 26, Wagner, the Nazi commander, asked the Norwegian Supplies Department for additional provisions for fourteen days, to be brought to the ship before it left port. The director of the department, realizing that the prisoners would need food, brought additional provisions down to the dock, including such Norwegian delicacies as sardines, kippered herring, fishcakes, and canned food. None of this food, however, reached the Jewish prisoners. It was all stolen by the Germans. On the voyage from Oslo to the German port of Stettin,[165] the prisoners were fed only bread, margarine, and thin soup.[166] There were 532 prisoners on the *Donau,* about one-fourth of the prewar Jewish population of Norway. They included an eight-week-old infant and an eighty-two-year-old woman.[167] Among the Norwegian Jews who died in German gas chambers were seventy-four children.

The trip to Stettin was a stormy one, lasting four days, with snow and fog alternating with gales. For several hours, the ship lay in the Øresund, the straits between Denmark and Sweden that connect the North Sea with the Baltic Sea. On one side of the Øresund lay the brightly lit city of Malmö in neutral Sweden and on the other lay blacked-out Copenhagen. Some of the prisoners considered trying to escape by jumping overboard, but none did. It is unlikely that any would have survived for more than a few minutes in the wintry sea. On November 30, the *Donau* reached Stettin, where the prisoners were loaded into cattle cars, the men and women separately, about sixty or seventy persons for each car. The train left Stettin at 5:12 p.m. and reached Auschwitz in Poland at 9:00 p.m. the following day. They received nothing to eat or drink during the 28-hour journey.[168]

Upon arrival at Auschwitz, 186 of the men were led away to become slave laborers. The remaining 346, consisting of all the women and children and the men who were considered too old or ill for slave labor, were immediately taken to the gas chambers. They were ordered to undress on the pretext that they would need to take a shower before going to a rest camp that had high standards of hygiene. Their shoes, clothing, eyeglasses, and such things as artificial limbs were collected. They were then forced to enter the gas chamber, where the naked people were pressed tightly together. Tablets of a chemical that produced poisonous prussic acid gas were thrown into the chamber, and death ensued within five to twelve minutes. The bodies of victims were cremated, but not before the gold fillings were broken out of their teeth.[169] The murder of the Jews was carried out with speed and ruthless efficiency. The Shoah records indicate that Elly Salomon died on December 1, 1942, the same evening the freight train from Stettin arrived at Auschwitz.

Despite the many recountings of the Holocaust during the past sixty years, it still takes an effort to imagine Elly Salomon's experience. When did it begin to dawn on her that she was about to die? Despite the persecution of the Norwegian Jews during the previous two and a half years, it is unlikely that before she was arrested she had any idea of the fate the Nazis were preparing for her. Was it when she saw the brutal scene at the dock in Oslo early in the morning on November 26, where the Jewish prisoners were no longer treated as human beings? Was it on board the *Donau*? Was it when she arrived at Stettin and was packed into a cattle car? Was it when she arrived at Auschwitz? Or was it when she finally entered the death chamber and the doors were shut? Like each of the six million Jews who died in the Holocaust, Elly suffered her own private terror and agony.

The fate of the Norwegian deportees was no secret. Although members of Elly's family did not know that she was one of the deportees on the *Donau*, very soon afterwards at least one of them had a good idea of what had happened to these unfortunate persons. On February 4, 1943, Elly's first cousin Max Salomon wrote from rural Sweden to his sister Gerda in the United States about the deportation of the Norwegian Jews. He wrote: "The whole family Seligmann were deported [from Norway] on that steamer. Probably they were all taken to Poland, and so far nobody ever returned from there. The old people are actually done away with, and the younger ones are worked to death as slaves. The whole thing is so utterly unbelievable and time and time again one has to ask oneself if it is not only a nightmare. I know nothing about the fate of Hans [Elly's brother] and Elly." Thus, in early 1943 the general outline of the Holocaust apparently was common knowledge in Sweden.

The arrests and deportation of Norwegian Jews continued after the sailing of the *Donau*. In February 1943, another 158 were deported from Oslo on the *S.S. Gotenland*. A few others were deported between 1941 and 1944.[170]

The deportations were accompanied by the theft of the deportees' property. On October 26, 1942, the same day as the mass arrests of Jewish men, the Quisling government adopted a law confiscating all property belonging to Jews, their spouses, and their children.[171] The Quisling government established a Liquidation Board for Confiscated Jewish Property for the purpose of carrying out the confiscation law. The Germans allowed the Norwegians to keep everything except for gold, silver, watches, and jewelry, which the Germans appropriated for themselves.[172] The property taken by the Norwegians was stored and then sold at a low price (or practically given away), with preference given to Norwegian soldiers who had joined the Nazi SS (the Hirden) or who had fought alongside the Germans on the Russian front. According to a Norwegian journalist, writing in 1995:

Regardless of whether it was the Germans who gave the initial orders, it was Norwegians who conducted the main part of the confiscation of Jewish property. It was a time for vultures, and valuables worth millions of kroner were taken. Nobody knows the exact value of the stolen goods.

. . .

It is a fact that Norwegians, including people who were not Nazis, profited the most from the Jewish tragedy.

. . .

The economic liquidation of the Norwegian Jews and what happened when they were supposed to be restituted after the war is a black hole in our national history.[173]

When Elly Salomon was arrested, the Norwegian authorities made a careful inventory of her property. Although her personal belongings were modest, it quickly became apparent that she owned substantial financial assets. In a letter to the Norwegian Finance Department, Andorf Lindahl, the officer of Quisling's NS party who was put in charge of her property, emphasized that the matter was of "special interest." According to Lindahl, Elly's total assets were worth 73,350.49 Norwegian kroner. This amount would have the purchasing power of at least $225,000 in 2004 U.S. dollars.[174] Most of these assets were in corporate shares, including shares of the Salomon Shoe Factory and of Danish and Swiss companies, which her father, Siegmund Salomon, had given her in 1939.

Lindahl expended great efforts to get his hands on Elly's property. It appears that either Elly or her father had placed some of her assets beyond Lindahl's reach in a Swiss bank account. But even with respect to her assets in Norway, Lindahl's rapacity was not entirely successful. There was a safe deposit box at the Kristiania Folkebank, which may have been in both Elly and Siegmund's names. Siegmund, it may be recalled, was living in Denmark at the time and had recovered his Danish citizenship in 1916. At first, the bank refused Lindahl's request to open the box, but Lindahl eventually succeeded in gaining access to it. In the box were two gold bars, each worth 5,208 kroner. The bank manager took the position that the gold bars belonged to Siegmund and therefore were not covered by the Norwegian confiscation law of October 26, 1942, whereas Lindahl argued that the gold had belonged to Elly and now were the property of the Norwegian government.

On April 30, 1943, five months after Elly's arrest and murder at Auschwitz, Lindahl wrote to Hauptsturmführer Wagner, asking him to resolve the matter and stating that the Norwegian dental association was interested in obtaining the gold bars because of the shortage of gold. The Germans were neither fooled nor deterred by such transparent duplicity. They simply confiscated the gold bars themselves, leaving Lindahl and the Norwegians government out in the cold.

In May 1945, the postwar Norwegian government established a Reparations Board for Confiscated Assets, with the responsibility of returning property to its rightful owners and of restoring the money equivalent of items that could not be traced.[175] The Reparations Board shamelessly accepted the false figures kept by the Quisling government in order to reject many Jewish claims and avoid paying other more than a fraction of their true value. In 1945,

Quisling's Liquidation Board handed over to the Reparations Board a list of Elly Salomon's stolen assets, and astonishingly valued them at only 11,219.46 kroner, or less than one-sixth of the value Quisling's officials had assigned to the stolen property in 1942. This figure purported to include the two gold bars and the shares of stock that she owned. It is unclear whether any restitution of even this lesser amount was ever made to her family.

Elly's personal belongings had been sold for 737 kroner after her death. After the war, a lawyer assigned to handle her case gave her brother Hans a check for the pitiful amount of 501.16 kroner. Presumably, the difference of 235.84 kroner represented the lawyer's fee and other expenses.

After the war, Hauptsturmführer Wagner, the German SS commander in Norway who was in charge of the deportation of the Norwegian Jews, was sentenced to death, but the penalty was reduced to twenty years in prison. Quisling and twenty-four other leaders were tried for murder, treason, and other crimes, and were executed in 1946. Ninety thousand other Norwegians — one out of every forty inhabitants — were investigated for treason or war crimes; of these, 18,000 received prison sentences and 28,000 were fined or deprived of their civil rights. Within a few years, the prison sentences were reduced, and in 1957 a general amnesty was declared.

So far as is known, the individuals directly responsible for the deportation of Elly and other Norwegian Jews did not pay heavily for their crimes. The case of Police Inspector Knut Røed is revealing. Røed was the highest ranking Norwegian officer present on the quay on November 26, 1942, when over 500 Norwegian Jews were loaded on the *S.S. Donau*, bound for Auschwitz; and in January 1943 he was placed in charge of implementing all anti-Jewish measures in Norway. He was a member of regular Norwegian State Police, not the Norwegian Nazi Security Police. In effect, however, he headed the Norwegian arm of the operations of Adolf Eichmann.

Røed tried to round up the Jews who had escaped the 1942 arrests; he wrote to hospitals to try to find out if they were harboring Jews who had suffered mental breakdowns. In September 1943, however, he resigned from the State Police, perhaps because he saw that Germany was bound to lose the war and that he was likely to be held accountable for his actions.

After the war, Røed was tried by a Norwegian court for war crimes, including his role in the action against the Jews. The prosecutor asked for a minimum sentence of three years, but on February 4, 1946, the jury acquitted him. The trial judge reversed the decision, on the ground that Røed's prominent role in the actions against the Jews could not be overlooked or excused. The case went to the Supreme Court, which canceled the jury verdict of acquittal and ordered the case to be retried. During the second trial, the Norwegian policeman who had been in charge of the reception of the arrested Jews on the quay testified that he had been greatly assisted by Inspector Røed. Nevertheless, on April 9, 1948, Røed was again found not guilty. The court found that his only purpose in carrying out the actions against the Jews was to camouflage his crucial work for the home front. This time, his acquittal was not appealed.

After his second acquittal, Røed (having changed his name to Rød) applied for reemployment with the Oslo

Metropolitan Police. His application was rejected on May 18, 1948. Rød then sued the Police Department for reinstatement. On September 10, 1948, the Oslo Town Court found in his favor. The Ministry of Justice appealed this decision to the Supreme Court, which upheld the Town Court's verdict, citing the lower court's rationale that he had joined Quisling's Nazi party in 1941 solely as camouflage for his work for the good of the nation. Furthermore, the court found that Rød's position in the State Police from 1941 to 1943 had made it possible for him to succeed in carrying out extraordinarily good work (this presumably included arresting and deporting Jews).

Knut Rød was reemployed by the Oslo Police on June 1, 1952 and continued working there until he retired on June 30, 1965. By that time, he had risen to become head of the crime squad. Upon his retirement, the Oslo police chief praised him for his services to the police for thirty-eight years (1927-65), including the war years, and described him as a highly experienced and competent policeman. Since Rød had been found not guilty in the two criminal trials, none of his subordinates was investigated or charged.[176]

Andorf Lindahl, the Norwegian official who was in charge of the theft of Elly's property, was arrested after the war. It is not known whether or not he was convicted of any crime.

Hans: Imprisonment and Escape

{1940-1945}

HANS SALOMON, the oldest son of Siegmund and Melitta Salomon, was born in Norway in 1902. The family moved to Copenhagen in 1913 when his father retired from active management of the Salomon Shoe Factory. For some years he worked in the shoe business in Copenhagen but he moved back to Norway during the 1930s.

In January 1939, while his father remained in Denmark, Hans and his mother bought a farm in the Valdres valley of Norway, a picturesque area surrounded by mountains reaching to 8,000 feet.[177] There Hans tried to establish a business as a distributor of Italian and English shoes. Around this time, he married Gunvor Petersen, a non-Jew twelve years younger than he, who was born in Sweden but had lived most of her life in Denmark.

In 1939, Hans and Gunvor went to live on the Valdres farm, and in March 1940 — two weeks before the German invasion of Norway — they were joined there by Hans's mother, Melitta, and his only sister, Elly. Gunvor was in the eighth month of pregnancy. Soon after the invasion, the farm was visited by a German, who asked some questions and then departed. Believing the man to be a spy or informer, they decided to leave the farm and take refuge in a small cabin in the mountains, where they stayed for a week. Then, accompanied by a young Jewish man who had joined them, they set out on foot through the snow-covered mountain passes for the Swedish border, over 150 miles away. By early June, they had reached a low-lying area near the border where the snow had melted and spring had arrived. There, under a tree in the forest, on June 6, 1940, Gunvor gave birth to Hanne, the first of her four children.

Two days later, the Norwegian forces who had been fighting the Germans in northern Norway surrendered. By this time, the young man who had accompanied them on their trek had managed to escape to Sweden. Hans and his family stayed about a week in a farm house with friendly local people and then headed again for the Swedish border, now accompanied by their newborn child. But the Swedish military officer at the frontier refused to let them enter the country and advised them to return to their homes.

At this time, whether Norwegian refugees were allowed to enter Sweden was largely a matter of chance: it depended on where they tried to enter and whether the Swedish official in charge was pro-German or sympathetic to refugees. Jews were not the only people refused entry. Even the Crown Princess of Norway, who was born and raised in Sweden, was turned back at the border by Swedish officials in early April 1940. On the other hand, Max Salomon and his sister Gerda Weill both managed to escape to Sweden, by different routes, a few days after the German invasion.

With help from local people, Hans and his family stayed hidden in a small hut near the Swedish border for three or four weeks, then returned to their farm by bus. Melitta left for Oslo, and shortly afterwards Elly joined her there. Sometime later, Melitta, who held Danish citizenship, was permitted to travel to Denmark; but Elly stayed in Oslo, where she would be arrested and deported two years later. Hans and Gunvor remained at the farm, where their second child, Leif, was born on November 27, 1941.

Although Hans and Gunvor were not harmed during the first two years of the German occupation, their situation was perilous. On several occasions they applied for exit visas to leave Norway, but their requests were turned down. In October 1942, Hans was arrested in the roundup of Jewish males by the Norwegian State Police and sent to the squalid Berg Concentration Camp near Tønsberg on the western shore of Oslo Fjord. Gunvor and her two small children stayed at the farm. Gunvor was now pregnant with her third child. Because Hans was married to a Christian, he was not deported on the *Donau* on November 26, 1942, but was held at Berg pending a resolution of his case.

As with his aunt Johanna, the question of Hans's citizenship was crucial. Hans would not have been deported to Auschwitz even if he had been considered a Norwegian citizen because he was married to a non-Jew; but he would have been interned at Berg for the remainder of the war, and the family's farm would have been subject to the decree of October 26, 1942 confiscating Jewish property.

Hans's father, Siegmund, born in Denmark, became a Norwegian citizen in the 1890s. When he left Norway with his family in 1913, he presumably lost his Norwegian citizenship and regained Danish citizenship. Hans was still a minor when the family moved to Denmark, so when his father became a Danish citizen, Hans's nationality changed too. Nevertheless, Hans and Gunvor held Norwegian passports and considered themselves Norwegian. Like Johanna, Hans had described himself as Norwegian on the questionnaire for Jews earlier in 1942. As a result, he was on the list of Jews whose property was subject to confiscation.

It is possible that Siegmund asked the Danish authorities to obtain the release of his son from the Norwegian prison on the ground that he was a Danish citizen. In any event, the Danish MFA took quick and effective action on Hans's behalf. They notified Schrøder, the Danish consul-general in Oslo, on January 27, 1943, that Hans and his family were Danish citizens and instructed Schrøder to request Hans's release from Berg prison and to assist the family in obtaining Norwegian exit visas and in applying for Danish entry visas. The following day, Schrøder requested the Norwegian Ministry of the Interior to investigate the matter "and, in the event that he [Hans] is actually in custody, to see to it that he, as a Danish citizen, is released from the internment camp."[178]

On February 13, the Ministry of the Interior ordered the State Police to release Hans, and two days later the State Police forwarded this order to the commander of the camp, a man named Wallestad. Nevertheless, Hans was not released, because, according to Wallestad, even while at the camp Hans continued to insist he was a Norwegian citizen; and Wallestad wanted to consult the head of the Security Police (the Norwegian SS) for further investigation. Even when the Norwegian State Police on February 19 ordered Wallestad to release Hans immediately, Wallestad continued to resist. Again, insistent pressure from Schrøder probably made the crucial difference. Schrøder called Deputy Commissioner Knut Røed of the Norwegian State Police (the same high-ranking Norwegian police officer who had turned Elly Salomon over to the Germans on the Oslo dock on November 26, 1942) and demanded to know why Hans had not been released.[179]

Hans was finally released from the Berg camp on February 22, allowed to catch a train to Oslo, and ordered to present himself to the State Police headquarters when he arrived there. He returned to his farm to pick up Gunvor and the children. Apparently, his assets had not been confiscated, since the German authorities permitted the waiving of this order in cases where a Jewish husband was detained in a concentration camp and a non-Jewish wife had to support herself.[180] The family then went by train to Gothenburg, where they lived until the end of the war. During his imprisonment, Hans had requested that since his wife was of Swedish origin they be permitted to go to Sweden rather than to Denmark.[181] Gunvor, who is now over ninety, remembers, however, that they were supposed to go to Denmark but got off the train in Sweden instead. This is supported by the wording of the order of the German Security Police releasing Hans, which refers to both Hans and Gunvor as Danish citizens.[182] On the other hand, it is at least questionable whether the Danish or the Swedish authorities would have allowed them to alter their destination; despite Gunvor's recollection, it seems possible that their request to go to Sweden was granted.

Hans and Gunvor had two more children, a daughter, Bodil, born in Sweden in April 1943; and a son, Finn, born in 1946. Melitta joined them in Gothenburg in October 1943; she and her youngest son Sven had escaped to Sweden in October 1943 along with her nephew Harald and his family. After the war, Hans and Gunvor returned to the farm in the Valdres for a short time, but they sold it in 1946 and went to live in Denmark, where Hans died in 1962. Gunvor and her two eldest children, Hanne and Leif, still live in Copenhagen. Melitta spent two years in the United States after the war with her musician sons Victor and Jarl, but returned to Denmark, where she died in 1958 at the age of seventy-nine.

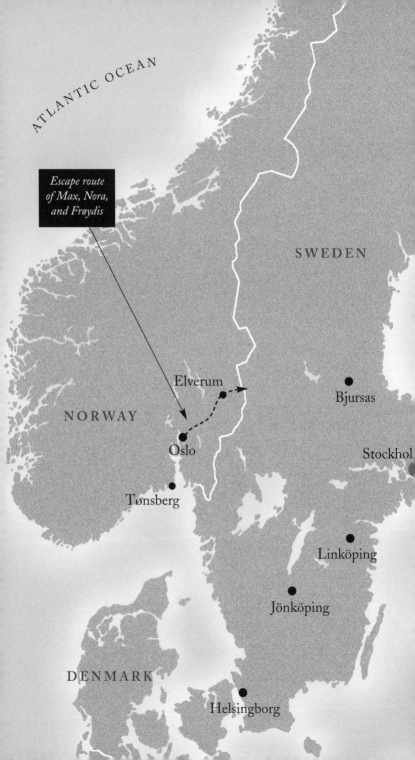

ATLANTIC OCEAN

SWEDEN

Escape route
of Max, Nora,
and Frøydis

Elverum

NORWAY

Bjursas

Oslo

Stockhol

Tønsberg

Linköping

Jönköping

DENMARK

Helsingborg

Max in Sweden

{1940-1945}

ON APRIL 9, 1940, Max, Johanna's oldest child, awoke to see German airplanes — visible from his home in Nordstrand — landing at the Oslo airport. Even before the German invasion, Max realized that the situation for a Jewish family in Norway was becoming dangerous, and he began thinking of leaving the country. By March 1, he had obtained from a friend in the Norwegian government named Hesselberg the Passerseddelen (pass permit) that would permit him, his wife Nora and his infant daughter Frøydis to go to Sweden. Nevertheless, the early-morning invasion six weeks later caught him by surprise. Unlike the great majority of Norway's 2,100 Jews, Max and Nora immediately decided to flee. This is how Frøydis relates her parents' story of the family's escape:

> My father had a friend at the department of justice, and this friend was able to give my parents the necessary papers to leave for Sweden. But first we left Oslo in my parents' small Austin for a farm some 140 kilometres north of Oslo. This farm belonged to some relatives of my father's friend at the department. My

father knew that the Germans were on their way to Oslo, and the only things my parents were able to bring with them was the necessary things for their baby – which was me. So they arrived at the farm with only the clothes they had on. The farmer and his family were very friendly, but after some days, the Germans reached the nearby town. There was only one thing to do: to move on to Sweden. The escape was uncomplicated I have been told. We drove the same way as the king and parliament had come by bus only hours before, and midway between the farm and Sweden were the ruins of the bombed bus in which the king had fled. Fortunately no one was killed. The king and his men got to Sweden, and so did we.

Although Frøydis is mistaken in believing that King Haakon escaped to Sweden, she is surely correct in stating that Max and his family took the same escape route from Oslo as the king. The Swedish government's policy was pro-German at the time, and it refused to give the king a guarantee of safe conduct back to Norway if he entered Swedish territory. Hoping in vain that Norway and its British and French allies might defeat the German invasion, the king and his government decided to remain in Norway.

At first they made their headquarters in Elverum, a town about 100 miles northeast of Oslo, where he rejected the German demand that he capitulate and accept the pro-Nazi government that Vidkun Quisling was attempting to establish. Pursued by the German army, on April 11 the king and his government made their way from Elverum to the tiny village of Nybergsund, only about twenty miles from the Swedish border. German bombers attacked Nybergsund, but at the first sight of the approaching planes the king and his advisers "retreated to a nearby forest where, standing in deep snow, they watched the German planes smash the hamlet to splinters. When the German planes had disappeared . . . , the king and his government continued their northward retreat, hoping to rally their countrymen along the way."[183]

The bombed bus that Frøydis remembers her parents telling her about may have been one of the results of this air raid.

King Haakon and the members of his government made their way to northern Norway, where the Norwegians, aided by a British-French expeditionary force, resisted the German invaders for two months. However, after the Germans invaded the Low Countries and France in May 1940, Norway became of secondary importance to the Allies and, despite some military successes around Narvik, they withdrew their forces. On June 7, King Haakon embarked with his ministers on the British cruiser *H.M.S Devonshire* from the northern Norwegian city of Tromsø, to set up a government in exile in London.[184]

It took courage and foresight for Max to flee Oslo within hours after the invasion, abandoning their home, their friends, and their possessions. Max and his sister Gerda, who also left immediately for Sweden, were among the few Jews who did so in 1940. Most of the Norwegian Jews who fled during the occupation did not attempt to escape until late 1942, when the Germans began arresting and deporting the remaining Jewish population of Norway.[185]

Max and Nora spent the remainder of the war in neutral Sweden. Because their lives were greatly circumscribed by the Swedish government, it is important to understand something about the evolution of Swedish policy toward refugees from Nazi persecution during the 1930s and 1940s. During the prewar period, Sweden admitted very few Jewish refugees from Nazi Germany. Even Fascist Portugal was more willing to accept refugees.[186]

Between the time of the Nazis' seizure of power in 1933 and the beginning of the war in 1939, Sweden granted residence permits to only about 3,000 Jews. The country's restrictive immigration policy was shaped by a combination of political expediency, economic concerns, anti-Semitism, and general xenophobic sentiment.[187]

The Swedish government's aim during the 1930s was not primarily to help refugees from Hitler but on the contrary to ensure that as few of them as possible were admitted into the country.[188]

Sweden did not wish to offend Germany, its principal trading partner and powerful neighbor, by accepting Jewish refugees. This attitude was strengthened by a concern that refugees from Hitler would compete with Swedish citizens for employment. According to one scholar, the Swedish *Utlänningsbyrån* (Foreigners' Bureau), the government agency with responsibility for refugee affairs, "often dealt with Jews in a manner characterized by xenophobia and antisemitism."[189] Furthermore, the members of the Jewish community in Sweden, which numbered about 7,000 in 1940, did not protest the restrictions on immigration, because they feared that the admission of more Jews into the country would result in increased anti-Semitism.[190]

During the 1930s, the Swedish government blatantly discriminated against Jewish immigrants. In 1938, restrictive rules were introduced for permits to settle in Sweden. In one notorious action, Sweden actually pressured the German government to stamp passports of German Jews with the letter "J."

Because Germans visiting Sweden did not require visas, a Jew carrying a German passport could enter Sweden freely. Knowing that German Jews entering the country were likely to want to stay there, Sweden sought a means of turning German Jews away without having to require all Germans to obtain visas, a step that neither government wanted. The Nazi German government therefore agreed to the Swedish request that all persons of German nationality who were defined as Jewish under the 1935 Nuremberg Laws would have their passports stamped with a large red "J."[191]

It should be kept in mind that during the 1930s the Nazi policy of persecuting the Jews had not yet evolved into a policy of exterminating them. Sweden's restrictive policy toward refugees began to change after the war began and the Nazi persecution of the Jews intensified.[192] Although Sweden continued to appease Germany, it did not have an official policy of barring the entry of Norwegian refugees, whether Jewish or not, during the turbulent days immediately following the German invasion. Whether or not a refugee was allowed into the country from Norway in April-June 1940 seems to have depended largely on the whim, or the political sentiments, of the particular border official. As we have seen, Hans Salomon and his family were turned back at the border in June 1940.

Despite its wish to appease Germany, the Swedish government made clear that it would resist an attack. On April 12, three days after the invasion of Denmark and Norway, the Swedish Prime Minister, Per Albin Hansson, made a radio address in which he said that it was possible that Germany had the same plans for Sweden as for the two other Scandinavian countries, and that if that occurred the Swedes would fight to the end with all means at their disposal.[193] Not knowing whether it too would be invaded, Sweden mobilized its armed forces, and soldiers could be seen everywhere when Max and Nora entered the country a few days after the invasion of Norway.

In April 1940, Max and Nora, armed with the papers that Max had the foresight to obtain from a Norwegian government official, were able to cross into neutral Sweden without difficulty. It is unlikely that the Swedish border guards knew or cared whether a Norwegian refugee was Jewish. Very few Jews fled Norway at that time and, besides, they were fellow Scandinavians. There was a sense of kinship among the Scandinavian countries that extended to Jewish refugees from Norway, at least if the particular Swedish officer at the border did not happen to be a Nazi sympathizer. It appears that Max and Nora were received with cordiality and sympathy by the border population and government officials.[194] They continued on to Dalälven, where friends took them in. Dalälven is a town about 150 miles northwest of Stockholm in an area famous for its enormous copper mines, which have been worked since the thirteenth century. Eventually, they made their way to Stockholm.

In 1940, Sweden's principal aim was to stay out of the

war, and this meant making a long series of concessions to Germany. In practice, in the early years of the war Sweden became "a non-combatant on the German side."[195] With Norway and Denmark under German control, Sweden was cut off from the West and ringed by the German army, and Germany was Sweden's only important trading partner. In June 1940, the Swedish government bowed to German pressure to allow German soldiers and war materials to cross Sweden by rail. Between 1940 and 1943, a total of about two million German soldiers traveled through Sweden on Swedish railroads to occupied Norway. After Germany invaded Russia in the summer of 1941, an entire army division was transferred through Sweden from Norway to Germany's ally, Finland.[196] Furthermore, in order to avoid provoking Germany, the Swedish government censored the press and theatrical productions to eliminate the expression of anti-German sentiments.[197]

Although Max and Nora were permitted to stay in Sweden, the Foreigners' Bureau placed severe restrictions on their lives. They received a residency permit, which had to be renewed every three months. During the years 1940-43, when German power and influence were at their peak, the private and working lives of Jewish refugees in Sweden were subjected to intense scrutiny and control by the police and security authorities. According to one historian:

> Frequent personal reports to the police authorities regarding social contacts and restrictions relating to residence, travel and check of personal correspondence were elements of this increased control, which affected not only Jews but also other refugees.[198]

Opportunities for employment for refugees were limited, particularly for a middle-aged businessman like Max (he was forty-two when he arrived in Sweden). He labored under three handicaps: he was a foreigner, a Jew, and a refugee. Many Swedish companies that did business with Nazi Germany fell into line with Germany's racial policies by refusing to hire Jews. To start a business, a foreigner had to obtain a permit from the government, and this was often an uncertain, humiliating, and lengthy process. The application had to be submitted to an administrative office, which included representatives of small business and industrial organizations and regional chambers of commerce. These offices often turned down applications submitted by Jews, although they usually masked their anti-Semitic attitudes by referring instead to the unemployment situation.[199]

The bright spot was that, with the outbreak of the war and the mobilization of Sweden's military forces, there began to be a shortage of manpower. Refugees were no longer regarded as a drain on the economy but rather a resource to be exploited. This was particularly true in occupations such as agriculture, which required physically trying manual labor.[200] Faced with very limited opportunities for employment, Max and his family went to live in Bjursås, a village not far from Dalälven, the town which had been their first stop in Sweden.

Max, who had never before worked as a physical laborer, obtained a working permit as a lumberjack in the forests around Bjursås. During the first years of their Swedish exile they were not allowed to travel outside the county in which Bjursås was located without a special permit, which was not easy to obtain. Travel restrictions were often imposed on refugees during the early years of the war: the Foreigners' Bureau sometimes placed refugees in sealed, cordoned-off areas of the country.[201] In September 1942, Max wrote to Gerda that he had not been allowed to visit Stockholm since the previous January, but, looking at the silver lining, he added that this meant that they were saving money on travel expenses.

For more than three years, Max and Nora lived on a farm in Bjursås. At first, they lived, with their baby, in a single room in the farmhouse, but they were allowed an additional room when their second child, Birgit, was born in 1941. It was a hard and strenuous life, but they seem to have thrived on it. Max adapted himself to his new line of work; he was proud to say that he was not ill for a single day during his five years in Sweden. In September 1942, Nora wrote to Gerda in America: "Our hands look like farmers' hands, our faces are sunburnt and hard, our children are running about all day long."

They had very little money and were largely dependent on their own efforts to feed themselves. There was enough food, and plenty of milk for the children. They grew their own vegetables, a task that Max, who loved gardening, enjoyed. For meat, they kept rabbits, which Max took care of in the morning before he went off to his day's work in the forest. In the evening, he brought in the firewood. For a time, his employer required him to live in a workmen's barracks, and he could only come home on Sundays. Work was not always available; in September 1942, he reported to Gerda that he had been working at odd jobs almost all the time, mostly in the woods. A month later, he wrote that he had no work because of the influx of able-bodied young Norwegian farm workers who had escaped to Sweden to escape being drafted by the Germans for slave labor.

Nora looked after the children and conserved fruits and vegetables. Before the harsh Swedish winter set in, they slaughtered their rabbits and preserved the meat. They even tried their hands at wine making — from white currants. She wrote exultantly to Gerda in New York in September 1942:

> Now the cellar is filled with lovely strawberries and juice of strawberries and gooseberries, red currents and raspberries and loganberries and beans and mushrooms. Now I might have a weeks time, then we'll start collecting 'tyttebaer' [lingonberries] and later on apples. After that we shall be kept busy about a whole week with getting the potatoes in. Everybody at the farmhouse who can walk will help with that work.

In 1941, they considered emigrating to the United States, as Gerda had done the previous year, and they applied for visas. However, by that time the difficulties of travel had become overwhelming. Japan had closed its borders to travelers in transit. Crossing the Atlantic by freighter from the Swedish port of Gothenburg ran the risk of being sunk by a German U-boat. Travel through Russia to Iran or India also seemed risky and uncertain. So they decided to stay in Sweden for the duration of the war.

On March 19, 1941, Max and Nora's second child was born. They named her Birgit Else Johanne. This was at a time when Germany ruled most of Europe, opposed only by Britain, and there seemed to be no future. It is a sign of the hopelessness of those days that Max's mother, Johanna, in occupied Norway and his brother, Harald, in occupied Denmark, both reacted not with joy or congratulations but with dismay at Max and Nora's decision to have a baby. Johanna wrote to Gerda shortly before Birgit was born: "Can you believe that Nora is going to have a baby?" and, a few days after the birth: "What do you think of Max's baby? How terrible to be bound to such an obligation." Max wrote: "Harald almost got a fit when he learned about the new baby, thinks we are optimists (or crazy)," adding sourly: "His own kid [Lilian] is always ill, which of course makes him a pessimist."

Max and Nora were sociable people, and they made many friends in Bjursås. According to Nora, Bjursås "society" consisted of "three clergymen, two retired station masters and the dowager [mother-in-law?] to one, a traveling silk salesman with his wife and two kids (the latter we are most together with) and a few other people." One night, they went to a party six kilometers from their home; they had to walk both ways in the winter night and did not get home until 3:30 a.m. Although there was rationing in Sweden during the war, food was plentiful. Nora wrote:

The most important [thing] at parties is the food. . . . I think there is still more variety in food at parties as there was at our finest parties at home." In December 1942, two and a half years after they had left Norway, Max wrote to Gerda: "We do not complain over our life here; I am still in the woods, it is quite a good and healthy job when one gets used to it; we have friends and small parties, healthy kids and enough to eat, but not much money, still we are managing. But 1943 may well become a strenuous year. I do hope the Nazis will be smashed by next Christmas.

They never felt that they were singled out or discriminated against because Max was Jewish, but they gave up having any Jewish identity and did their best to blend in with the local population. Replying to a letter from Gerda in which Gerda apparently had asked whether they used their Jewish-sounding name in Bjursås, Nora wrote:

I had to laugh when I read your few words about not mentioning Max's name. I would never have dreamt that you could go that way. As a matter of fact I may tell you that, although everyone here knows our name, no-one is thinking of 'race.' Birgit got baptized right after her birth and we are quite pally (even Max) with the clergyman of this place.

In fact, they became so attached to Bjursås and their friends there that, more than a year after they left the village for good, they returned for a two-and-a-half-week vacation. After the war, their son, Robert, visited Bjursås on his summer vacations; and friends from Bjursås visited them in Norway. The visits became so frequent, Robert recalls, that Nora would look out of the window of their Oslo home and sigh resignedly: "Another car from Sweden!"

Even though Max and Nora were living in a remote Swedish village, they were well informed about what was happening in Norway. They read Norwegian- and English-language newspapers, and they also learned of the events in Norway by word of mouth. A steady stream of refugees crossed the border into Sweden. In all, Sweden accepted 50,000 Norwegian refugees during the war.[202]

The arrest and deportation of the Norwegian Jews in October and November 1942 was described in horrifying detail in the Swedish press and by clergymen in the churches.[203] It created an enormous storm of indignation. On December 13, 1942, Max wrote a detailed letter to Gerda in New York, describing these shocking events with great accuracy:

> One night all the men between 16 and 65 were arrested and sent to concentration camps. At the same time a decree was issued that all property belonging to Jews was to be seized. Some weeks later all the families, not previously arrested were rounded up and taken to a large German steamer in the docks. The men were taken from the concentration camp and brought aboard the same steamer, and all were deported, presumably to Poland. Nobody was allowed to take along any property, but they were told to bring food for 4 days. The most shocking details have been known here; the clergy and the people of Norway are reacting violently, also the clergy and some of the papers here, but alas it will not help the poor victims, I am afraid we know quite a few of them personally.

Max could not know at the time that his first cousin, Elly Salomon, was one of the victims of the Nazi terror, or that she had been killed at Auschwitz twelve days before he wrote this letter.

Beginning in 1942, the Swedish government gradually eased its refugee policy. The turning point in the change of attitude, both for the authorities and for public opinion, came with the German deportation of the Norwegian Jews. One result of this change in policy was that the work and travel restrictions that the Swedish government had placed on Max and his family were eased and eventually removed. Max was able to end his labors in the forests and to become an administrator of Norwegian refugees in Sweden. As a result, he discovered latent abilities in himself that he never before had an opportunity to use. Despite the hardships Max and his family endured, the war years were good for him.

Max had never enjoyed being a businessman and had not been successful in that role during the prewar years; now circumstances enabled him to work as an administrator for a publicly desirable cause in which he believed. Even while living in Bjursås, he made many friends and contacts through the Norwegian-Swedish Friendship Circle, in which he became an active member. He began giving lectures to raise money for a home for Norwegian refugees. Nora was an adoring wife, but there is every reason to believe that what she wrote about her husband to Gerda was no more than the truth:

> I must say you may be proud of your brother. He
> delivered a very good lecture both at Sagmyra and
> here at Bjursås. People were astonished and thought
> he had never done anything else in his life but
> holding lectures. He also looked fine with his
> sunburnt face and the grey hair.

Max's lectures were highly successful; one was attended by 300 to 400 people. In early 1943, he was allowed to travel to Stockholm to attend a meeting where he read Norwegian poems to an audience.

By that time, Swedish neutrality was no longer leaning in favor of Germany. As one scholar has observed: "From almost the beginning of the war to the end, [Swedish neutrality] swung back and forth like a pendulum; first in favor of Germany, then back towards the middle again where the Swedes wished it to be, and then in the latter part of the war, off center again in favor of the Allies."[204] By early 1943, after the Battles of Stalingrad and El Alemain, an eventual Allied victory seemed inevitable, and Sweden no longer felt that appeasement of Germany was essential to the country's security. Another important factor was that, by then, knowledge of the Holocaust was widespread, and Swedish public opinion had swung to sympathy with Jewish refugees. This change was a key factor in causing Sweden to announce publicly in October 1943 that it would give asylum to all the Danish Jews.[205]

These events affected the policy of the Foreigners' Bureau, which relaxed the work and travel restrictions that it had placed on refugees. In 1943, the Bureau permitted the family, which now included Robert, who was born that year, to leave Bjursås and move to the southern Swedish city of Jönköping. In January 1944, Max was appointed district representative in two Swedish provinces for the Refugee Office in Stockholm. The work was demanding, but he was well suited for it.

The next sixteen months, until the end of the war, may have been the most satisfying and productive of Max's life.

For the first time, he was able to exercise his talents as an administrator. His job gave him a great deal of authority over the Norwegian refugees under his jurisdiction. He had to stay informed about their living conditions, attend weddings and funerals, provide them with entertainment, obtain work for the able and assistance for the needy, take sick people to the hospital, report on criminals, keep a record of all these events, and submit reports to the authorities in Stockholm. He wrote to Gerda from Jönköping in July 1944:

> I have an office in this town and one or two assistants always working with me. It means lots and lots of work, and quite a bit of travelling in my territory. Sometimes it is rather trying helping all the refugees with their multitude of troubles and problems, but on the whole I find it very interesting work, and I do not mind working long hours and often part of Sundays as well. . . . I meet all sorts of people and all sorts of problems. One has got to act as an adviser, dole officer, supervisor, reporter, travel agency, counsel, doing even in some degree police and military police work. The pay is not too bad, and we manage nicely.

Even in Jönköping, Max continued to indulge in his love of gardening. He leased a piece of land and spent his spare time digging and planting. Max made a monthly salary of 500 Swedish kroner. It is practically impossible to estimate the equivalent of this amount in present-day purchasing power.[206] Suffice to say that Max and Nora felt that they had never lived so well before. Max continued working for the Norwegian refugee organization until he and his family returned to Norway shortly after the end of the war, along with the other Norwegian Jewish refugees who had been living in exile in Sweden.

*Gerda with Dorrit in Far Rockaway, New York,
around 1943.*

Gerda Escapes
to America

—•—

{1940-1945}

GERDA WEILL, Johanna's elder daughter, was a sweet
and loving woman. Born the daughter of a well-to-do
manufacturer, she lived a privileged life for her first forty-
one years. When the Germans invaded Norway in 1940,
she discovered in herself the courage, intelligence, good
judgment, and aggressiveness that the unprecedented situation demanded. Taking what must have seemed an enormous risk, she escaped with her daughter within days after
the invasion. She spent the remainder of her life in the
United States, where she was forced to adjust to a very
modest standard of living. During all the time I knew her,
I never once heard her complain about or regret her
reduced circumstances or boast about the higher social status and much more comfortable life she had enjoyed before
the war.

In early April 1940, when a German invasion seemed
imminent, Gerda was on a skiing vacation in Norway,
while her five-year-old daughter, Dorrit, was staying with
Johanna in Voksenlia. About the time of the invasion, she
returned to Voksenlia. The urgent question Gerda had to
decide was whether to stay or flee to Sweden. Johanna's

friend, Sverre Helliksen, tried to persuade Gerda to stay, telling her that the Germans would do her no harm. But Gerda had lived in Berlin in the early days of the Hitler regime, and she had no illusions about German intentions toward the Jews. In 1940, the Germans had not yet begun their program to exterminate the Jews, but the Nuremburg laws of September 1935 had deprived German Jews of their civil rights, and the pogrom known as "Kristallnacht" in November 1938 had demonstrated the Nazi government's capacity for organized anti-Semitic violence. Gerda was determined to leave Norway with her daughter if she could.

On April 11, the second day after the invasion, the German authorities, who had by then taken control of Oslo, ordered all nationals of countries with which Germany was at war to report to the police.[207] As the former wife of a British citizen, Gerda held a British passport and was arguably subject to this order. Unlike her mother, Gerda did not believe Helliksen's advice. Instead of waiting around to see what would happen, she acted made up her mind to escape to Sweden as quickly as possible.

Helliksen's role here was ambivalent. His sympathies were pro-German, but he was also a family friend of the Salomons. Once Gerda made her decision to leave Norway, Helliksen told her that she must do so immediately. Tomorrow would be too late. Helliksen was correct: the trains to Sweden ran for only two days after the invasion.[208] Although the Germans occupied Oslo on the first day of the invasion, April 9, for a few days after that they did not yet control the surrounding countryside. During this short period of uncertainty and chaos, it was possible for a determined person to escape the country by rail.

The story of Gerda's escape and long journey was told to me many years later by Dorrit, who was five years old at the time. Although Dorrit could not possibly have remembered many of the details of her long voyage, Gerda told her about it so many times that it was etched into her memory.

While many people were fleeing Oslo in panic, Gerda took a suburban train into the city with Dorrit and withdrew her money from a bank account. The two then went back to the Oslo railroad station, where a German guard at the entrance demanded in German to see Gerda's passport. Pretending not to understand him, she brushed past him. She heard the soldier say in German to his companion, "Crazy woman. They'll arrest her inside." Indeed, on the station platform from which the train to Sweden was about to leave, soldiers at the other end of the train were leading away a group of people whom they had just arrested and taken off the train. Thinking quickly, Gerda realized that this was a stroke of luck for her and Dorrit, because it meant that the German soldiers had already examined the passports of the passengers and had arrested enemy aliens and others whom they considered undesirable. Correctly assuming that the soldiers would not search the train again before it left, Gerda boarded the train with her daughter, and very soon the train started, bound for the Swedish border.

As may be expected, there was great uncertainty and fear in Norway immediately after the German invasion. Although the king and his government had fled Oslo, it was with the aim of continuing the fight against the Germans. An attempt by a company of German paratroopers to capture the king at Elverum, north of Oslo, had failed and its leader had been killed.[209] The king refused to recognize the Nazi collaborator Vidkun Quisling as prime minister and told the government leaders who were with him at Elverum that he would abdicate if the government agreed to Germans' demand that the Norwegian army lay down its arms. Since the elected ministers supported the king's repudiation of Quisling and the Norwegian army was still intact, there was still hope that, with the assistance of British and French expeditionary forces, it could repel the invaders.

The Norwegians, however, feared they were being betrayed by German spies. During summers before the war, members of the Nazi Youth Movement had visited Norway by the thousands, sketching and photographing buildings and installations. It is possible that many of these supposed tourists were among the German soldiers who invaded Norway in 1940. Furthermore, during the time of suffering and hunger in Germany immediately after the 1914-18 war, many Norwegian families had taken homeless German children into their homes, taught them Norwegian, and raised them with their own families. Before the second World War began, Hitler ordered these children (whom the Norwegians for some reason called *Wienerbarn,* or Viennese children) to return to Germany. Once there, the Nazi rulers told them that they would be sent back to Norway in order to assist that country to resist an Allied invasion. When they learned that they were being sent back in order to help the Germans take over the control of Norway and thus to betray the country in which they had been brought up, some of them reportedly committed suicide. Many, however, obeyed orders and returned to Norway as "a fifth column."[210]

It is not clear how much truth there was to the stories about the *Wienerbarn*. The important thing was that many Norwegians believed that these Norwegian-speaking Germans were now among the German soldiers invading their country, or were quietly entering the country from Sweden in civilian clothes in order help the invaders. The idea that they were being betrayed by those whom they had helped in their time of need angered the Norwegians more than almost anything else about the invasion.[211] Thus, during the first days of the German occupation, there was widespread belief in Norway that Norwegian-speaking infiltrators were present in the country.

Gerda and Dorrit, Stockholm, June 1940.

When Gerda and Dorrit settled down in a compartment on the Swedish-bound train, the other occupant of their compartment was a man who spoke to Dorrit. She climbed onto his lap and began telling him how they were escaping from Norway. For some reason, Gerda suspected that he was a German spy. Leaving the compartment, she found a conductor and told him she thought there was a German spy in her compartment. To her surprise, the conductor replied that there were several spies on the train, but that they did not know that the Norwegian army still controlled (or had recaptured) the place on the border where the train was to cross into Sweden. This turned out to be true.

When the train reached the border, Norwegian soldiers came on board and searched the train. It turned out that Gerda's suspicions were well founded: the man who had befriended Dorrit carried a German passport. The Norwegians took him and other Germans off the train. Gerda wondered what happened to them. Dorrit told me she remembered hearing shots as she sat with her mother in the train, so it is possible that the Norwegians summarily executed them. The train then crossed the border into Sweden and safety. Several teen-aged Norwegian boys escaped on the same train by riding under the railroad cars. Dorrit said she thought this was the last train to Sweden before the Germans took complete control of the border in southern Norway.

Despite Sweden's pro-German policy in 1940, it accepted many, if not most, refugees from Norway during the first days of the German invasion.[212] Sigrid Undset, the Nobel-winning Norwegian novelist, whose books were banned in Germany because she had spoken out against the Nazi regime, escaped with her son from northern Norway to Sweden over a mountain road a few weeks later. She wrote:

> The customs inspection was painless, although none of us had passes or, on the whole, anything resembling papers. . . . The [Swedish] officers and soldiers all did what they could to be helpful and pleasant. Only an occasional small local official could not hide his nervousness because his district was being overrun by such dangerous people as Norwegian refugees must be and gave vent to his irritation at the situation.[213]

When Gerda and Dorrit arrived in Stockholm, they discovered that Max, Nora, and their infant daughter Frøydis were among the Norwegian refugees who had already arrived there. Gerda said later that she had had a dream that Max had escaped. Max told her that he and his family planned to stay in Sweden, but Gerda had already decided to go to the United States, via Russia, Japan, and Canada, a route taken by a number of other refugees from Norway. She made the decision against the advice of Johanna, who wrote to her in June from Norway: "Another option [is] traveling [to the United States] via Russia-Siberia − 21 days by train − nobody can stand that!" As usual, Gerda ignored her mother's advice and used her own judgment.

One might imagine that this was a time of great anxiety and stress for Gerda and Dorrit, but that does not seem to have been the case, at least during the early part of the journey. For Dorrit, the long voyage from Norway to the United States was a great adventure. Gerda too seems to have enjoyed the journey, treating it as an adventurous vacation. Nevertheless, in an expressive photograph of them taken in Vancouver (presumably by a professional street photographer) in December 1940, signs of strain show clearly on Gerda's face.

They spent six months in Sweden, staying outside Stockholm with people they had just met. While she was there, Gerda took lessons jumping (not diving) into a swimming pool from a high diving board and received some kind of certificate for the skill she had acquired. She even climbed up to the diving board with her five-year-old daughter to show her how high it was. Gerda was unfailingly cheerful throughout an experience that a less sanguine person might have considered a harrowing ordeal. When Dorrit, dying of cancer in the summer of 2001, talked about the stay in Sweden and the long trip to the United States, she still remembered the experience as a fascinating and on the whole enjoyable adventure.

The next step of their journey took them to the Soviet Union, which had signed a pact with Nazi Germany in 1939 and was for the time being at peace with its neighbors. In October 1940, they flew from Stockholm to Moscow in a small Russian plane. On the plane a little dog came and sat on Dorrit's lap. The air must have been turbulent, because pretty soon both Dorrit and the dog threw up. An attendant offered her a piece of lemon to suck to prevent nausea, but Gerda wouldn't let her have it because it was dirty.

While in Sweden, Gerda had learned that any consumer goods could be sold in Russia, so she took the wise step of buying a number of wristwatches before leaving Sweden. In Moscow, they found a government-run office where consumer goods could legally be sold. Dorrit remembered going there with watches strapped up and down her arms. When Gerda saw that in Moscow anything at all could be sold, she brought over one of her nightgowns, which was eagerly snapped up as an "evening gown." The proceeds from these sales helped finance their train trip across Siberia.

Moscow, like all the Soviet Union, was indescribably poor and filthy. Unfortunately, Gerda did not keep a diary of the trip; but Sigrid Undset, who had made the same journey a few months earlier, described the scene vividly in a book she wrote after reaching the United States:

> In all Russia I did not see one woman with leather shoes on her feet. The children were generally barelegged and dressed in washed-out little bloomers and nothing more. But they all looked well, brown-legged, and not thin enough to hurt.
>
> . . .
>
> [B]elow the masses of uniformly poor and neglected-looking people in Moscow we now and then had an unpleasant glimpse of a pariah population, people whom the system of government had placed outside the social order, who have no right to be wherever they may be, who have nothing to live on except the alms they can get by begging. And they seemed a concentration of misery, a good deal worse than the worst I have seen anywhere else. Pressed against a wall where the stream of people flowed past hung these bundles of rags, mostly old women, their skin a crusty black from filth and houseless living, their hair green from dirt or mold; some forlorn children begged, too.

. . .

[T]here was literally not a thing in all Moscow which we could buy.[214]

Gerda and Dorrit stayed in Moscow for a few weeks, in a hotel in Red Square, where dancers entertained them every night. There, they met other Norwegian refugees en route to the United States.

The next leg of Gerda and Dorrit's journey was a two-week train ride on the Trans-Siberian Railway from Moscow to Vladivostok. Although they had a sleeping compartment, they had to share it with another woman and a man. They each had their own bunk. Although the railroad cars must have been the last word in train luxury when the railroad was built in the early 1900s, it was apparent that nothing had been done since then to keep them in working order. Nevertheless, they were roomy and substantial.

Food was available on the train and at the railway stations where they stopped. The only vegetable they could get was borscht (beet soup), and understandably Dorrit tired of it. At every train stop, ragged children and women selling berries swarmed into the dining-car. The berries were dirty and mostly unripe, but the dining car staff washed them and served them. This is what Undset wrote about the trans-Siberian journey in the summer of 1940:

> All the food we were served was taken on board at Moscow; no arrangements had been made whereby new supplies could be taken on at places along the way. So the meat smelled and tasted worse day by day. Worst of all was the lack of vegetables – a little

shredded white cabbage in a kind of meat soup was
all there was. Instead of potatoes we got dark-gray
macaroni cooked into a kind of porridge. The dessert,
cheesecakes, I renounced after the first attempt. They
smelled – and presumably tasted – like the stuff
babies belch when they have drunk too much milk.[215]

Nevertheless, it was an exciting experience for Dorrit,
in large part because almost everybody she and Gerda met
and traveled with was friendly. Gerda, who loved licorice,
broke a tooth on a piece of it, and couldn't get it fixed until
she reached America; but this mishap was more inconven-
ient than painful.

The train ride ended in Vladivostok, the major Soviet
port on the Sea of Japan. The city is built along low heights
around a wide, beautiful bay. Despite its picturesque site,
Vladivoskok made Moscow and the other cities of Russia
that they had passed seem almost well regulated and clean.
According to Undset, the city was beyond description. At
that time, most of the imports to the Soviet Union from
the United States and Japan arrived through Vladivostok.
Large quantities of wares were piled up on piers and open
squares and along the streets – wherever they happened to
be dumped. Undset wrote: "It looked as if they were left
lying there until they went to rack and ruin. We passed
mountains of radiator parts . . . ; they were rusted together
into great rufous mountains of scrap iron."[216]

After a week in Vladivostok, Gerda and Dorrit traveled
to Japan on a small ship. In contrast to Russia, Japan was
clean and full of consumer goods, much of it sold in quaint
little shops. During the three weeks they spent in Tokyo,
Gerda shopped. Among the things she bought were two

kimonos, silk to make a dress for herself, two dolls, a Japanese stringed instrument, and (to make up for the absence of fresh fruit in Russia) a huge bag of oranges. She also bought an elegant, slightly curved silver cigaret case, with pictures of Mount Fuji, a pagoda, and sailboats etched in color on both the outside and inside, which she gave to me in May 1941 as a bar mitzvah present. Although the colors on the outside of the case have faded, the inside is still as beautiful as it was sixty-five years ago. So Gerda, on her arduous journey more than halfway around the world, was thinking of her nephew in New York. Today, we might say that a cigaret case was an inappropriate gift for a thirteen-year-old. Nevertheless, it was — and still is — a gorgeous souvenir of prewar Japan and, more importantly, of my Aunt Gerda.

Gerda and Dorrit with a Japanese man and children,
Tokyo, December 1940.

In December 1940, when Gerda and Dorrit were in Japan, Pearl Harbor still lay a year in the future, but the country had been at war in Manchuria and China for a decade and was preparing for war against the United States. Relations between Japan and the United States had already become hostile. Dorrit remembered seeing violent demonstrators hurling excrement at the windows of the American Embassy in Tokyo. The brutalizing effects of Japan's Asian war and growing militarism were felt in daily life. People were so afraid of the police that it was common for a thief to kill himself if there was a danger of being arrested. Hostility to foreigners, at least those who spoke English, was increasing.[217]

Nevertheless, Gerda and Dorrit found Japan enchanting. At one point, Dorrit made friends with some children who pointed to her shoes, suggesting she take them off and come inside, which she did. A whole troop of children came to their hotel to play with her. Because Dorrit had blonde hair, she was a real curiosity to the Japanese children. The boys carried their baby brothers and sisters in backpacks. When the boys played soccer they put the backpacks down; and Dorrit circulated around the backpacks and played with the babies.

Gerda and Dorrit had a stormy voyage across the Pacific to Vancouver, where they stayed for three months, waiting to obtain a visa to enter the United States. There, Dorrit first learned to speak English. Later, Dorrit told her mother that she wished they had stayed in Vancouver instead of going on to New York. In view of the hardships they endured during the years that followed, this is completely understandable. There were many Norwegians in Vancouver, some of whom had made the same journey from

Norway, and a real sense of community existed among them. Gerda wrote to her mother, living in occupied Norway, that they were happy in Vancouver. The United States, however, was Gerda's goal and as soon as they obtained the necessary visas they continued on, arriving in New York in the early spring of 1941, almost exactly a year after they had fled Norway.

Gerda and Dorrit in Vancouver, December 1940.

In New York, Gerda found herself in a difficult position. She was forty-two years old, with very little money and no practical skills or working experience, and with a small daughter to look after. The only people Gerda knew in New York were her sister and brother-in-law, Jack and Grete Poser (my parents), who at the time were living in an eight-room duplex apartment on Riverside Drive.

Gerda may have expected to be welcomed with open arms by Jack and Grete, but she was to be disappointed in this. There were several reasons why she could not expect much help from them. Jack felt that there was no room because, in addition to themselves and their three children, Jack's two nieces from England were living in the apartment. Grete had little or no money of her own, and it is unlikely that Jack had any interest in providing Gerda and Dorrit with financial support, other than perhaps for their immediate needs when they first arrived. Besides, Grete was too involved in her own severe emotional problems — and perhaps in her own social life — to be of much help. Jack ruled the family; Grete did not make the decisions. Whatever the reasons, Jack and Grete provided little hospitality to Gerda and Dorrit.

Gerda was determined to support herself and not become a dependent "poor relation," even if the Posers had been willing to support her. She needed a job, and, with her lack of working experience and skills, the only kind of position she could get in New York at that time was as a domestic servant. Incredibly, there apparently was even some talk of her working as a servant in her sister's house, for Johanna wrote to her sometime in 1941:

Do you have any work prospects? Even though Grete could offer you a job in her house, I think you should get a position with someone you don't know; as you would be much more independent that way, and it may last for a long period of time.

She may have actually worked for Grete for a short time. In early 1943, Nora, her sister-in-law, wrote to Gerda: "I wonder whether you are still working at Grete's or whether you have found a new post." Soon, however, Gerda took a job as a nursemaid in Manhattan, and later as a housemaid for a family in Connecticut, who allowed Dorrit to stay with her. But that did not last long, and Gerda had to face the fact that she it was impossible for her to work at a fulltime job and also take care of Dorrit. Meanwhile, she was receiving a stream of advice from Johanna, who wrote to her in August 1941:

I could not fall asleep, and then I thought of you and the situation you have ended up in. Grete wouldn't be able to handle any more children around her, so I am afraid you must decide to place Dorrit in a boarding school for low-income families. It will be impossible for you to make any money as long as you need to look after the child at all times. As soon as the [summer] break is over, I think you should place her in a suitable institution. Then you can go look for a job. After all, you cannot simply bide your time until you have spent all your money.

At first, Gerda left Dorrit unattended while she was at work. However, after Dorrit twice was hit by a car (fortunately not suffering any real injuries), Gerda decided that she would have to send her away to a boarding school. Dorrit first attended a Norwegian children's home in Brooklyn, and then was sent to the Graham School in Hastings-on-Hudson, about thirty miles north of New York City. Dorrit did not remember these places as being too bad. Johanna, writing from occupied Norway in September 1941, as usual provided Gerda with detailed advice on how to bring up her daughter:

> I hear you have been busy getting Dorrit into school.
> I suppose she has moved in there by now? I am sure
> you both feel the void; after all, you have been
> inseparable for a year and a half. Let's just hope
> Dorrit will be happy there and not miss her mother. .
> . . Have you notified the school administrators that
> Dorrit must have some fruit daily as a digestive aid?

A month later, Johanna wrote:

> I have thought a lot about Dorrit and how she will
> like it at the Graham School. I am not surprised
> when she says she doesn't like it there. The child
> needs time to settle into her changed conditions first.
> So far, she has only been spoiled by her mother and
> everybody else around her. Dear Gerda, don't be
> lenient and take her out of school, because that would
> ruin everything for both yourself and the child.
>   Don't ask her how she likes it there; tell her how
> lucky she is to be out in the fresh air with all the
> other kids. We are not raising our children for
> ourselves, but for the world. I can imagine that you

felt lonely once she was gone and immediately jumped at the first [illegible] that presented itself. I hope you will have more luck next time. Working day and night at that is too much for you. The fact that you cannot visit Dorrit more often than once every two weeks is probably a good thing, she is supposed to feel totally at home there.

In late 1941, probably because she could not afford the Graham School, Gerda put Dorrit into an orphanage run by Orthodox Jews, which must have been considerably less expensive. By that time, Johanna and Gerda could no longer write to each other because the United States and Germany were at war, but we can infer from Johanna's later letters that she, though probably knowing nothing about the conditions there, approved of Gerda's decision to send her to the orphanage. Nevertheless, it was a frightful place, very reminiscent of Dotheboys Hall, the orphanage in Charles Dickens's *Nicholas Nickleby*, and it blighted Dorrit's childhood and created in her a lasting resentment against her Aunt Grete, who had the financial means to help support Gerda and Dorrit, and even against her mother.

When Dorrit first entered the orphanage, it was located in Manhattan, behind high walls, but it soon moved to Far Rockaway, a distant part of the city and a long subway ride from the area of Brooklyn where Gerda lived. The people who ran the orphanage were tyrannical and nasty. Dorrit was required to work very hard (this at the age of eight). Before breakfast, she had to set the table for sixty persons. She also had to look after babies. Gerda could only visit her once every two weeks and when she did she was not allowed even to take her outside for a walk. Nor was

Dorrit permitted to accompany her mother on her two-week summer vacations. Gerda worried that Dorrit would eventually become a complete stranger to her.

Dorrit spent nearly four years in the Jewish orphanage, while most of the time Gerda worked as a servant in people's homes. According to Dorrit, they were terrible years. Nevertheless, in 1944 Johanna, having escaped to Sweden and now again able to correspond with Gerda, continued to provide Gerda with advice on how to treat her daughter; she advised Gerda to leave her nine-year-old daughter in the orphanage for another three years:

> It is still too early for you to have Dorrit come and stay with you; what would the child do all by herself when you are at work? She would get bored and do stupid things. She still needs somebody to look after her, and you are saying yourself that she is in good hands where she is.
>
> With regard to Dorrit, I fully understand that you want her to live with you, but you must also understand how many hours you are away from home. Who would take care of her when she returns from school; she is such a lively child who would get bored and miss her classmates. No, I think she should stay where she is until she reaches 12 years of age.
>
> I am pleased to know that you are earning your keep and even have some money left over to put aside. As you wrote, the only problem is to get Dorrit back home, and I fully understand that. It really pained me to read that she has become so silent; but it is a good thing she is so sensible. Just let the entire matter rest until the war is over. Now that we have

been waiting for years, we can surely wait another few months. I am sure Grete will send her nieces home then, and who knows? Perhaps she will think that Dorrit would make for a good play mate for Elizabeth and take her in, just like she did with her other relatives.

To think that my Gerda one day would have to support her child and herself! That is truly commendable. Who would have thought so when you were a young girl?

Despite Johanna's hopes that Jack and Grete would take Dorrit in, they do not seem to have been particularly interested in Dorrit's welfare. Although they must have known something about Dorrit's life in the orphanage, they did not provide the financial assistance that could have enabled her to go to a decent (or less indecent) boarding school. In October 1942, Max Salomon, Gerda's brother, wrote to her from Sweden: "I note what you wrote about Grete's attitude when Dodo was ill, it was all rather disgusting." And Nora, Max's wife, wrote: "I am so glad, dear Gerda, that you can manage on your own. It would have been too horrid if you had been dependent on Grete and Jack." Since I do not have any of the letters that Gerda wrote to Max, I do not know what specific episode caused Max and Nora's comments; but one can assume that they were critical of Jack and Grete's apparent indifference to Dorrit's well-being.

Meanwhile, Gerda, determined to cease working as a domestic servant, took a course that qualified her to become an x-ray technician, and in 1943 she received her license. She would visit Jack and Grete on the weekends, and when she told Jack that she had enrolled in the x-ray course, he showed a mixture of admiration and contempt. This was consistent with the belittling attitude that he sometimes displayed toward family members, which can be summarized as: "What can you possibly be capable of doing?" On the other hand, he wrote to Max at about this time that he admired Gerda and that he had never believed that Gerda would be able to manage so well and be so "businesslike." Fortunately, Gerda ignored his doubts about her ability, just as she had ignored Helliksen's advice to stay in Norway in 1940 when the Germans invaded the country. She supported herself as an x-ray technician for the remaining three decades of her working life, living in the Bay Ridge area of Brooklyn, where she felt comfortable because it was populated largely by Norwegians.

Harald in his uniform as a driver for the Danish Brigade, with Else and Lilian shortly after the liberation of Denmark, May 1945.

Harald and the
Danish Rescue

{1943-1945}

AT THE TIME OF THE GERMAN INVASION, approximately 8,000 Jews lived in Denmark, including about 1,500 refugees who had fled Nazi Germany during the 1930s. Most of the Danish Jews were assimilated into Danish cultural and social life. Many of them, including Harald Salomon, had married non-Jews. Harald, his wife Else, their ten-year-old daughter Lilian, and Harald's mother Johanna, were among the Danish Jews and their non-Jewish spouses who fled Denmark when the Nazi German government decided to deport and murder the Danish Jews. However, Harald, Else, and Lilian's escape was more dangerous and harrowing than the experience of most of the other escapees.

The rescue of the Danish Jews is one of the great legends of the twentieth century. It is a unique episode in the history of the Holocaust, "a single beam of light from an otherwise dark continent."[218] While the non-Jewish populations of other German-occupied countries stood by while the Jews were rounded up and deported — or actively assisted the Germans — the Danes united to save most of their Jewish compatriots from the gas chambers.

When the Germans invaded Denmark on April 9, 1940, the Danish armed forces put up virtually no resistance. The Danish government accepted at face value Germany's assurance that it did not intend to encroach upon Denmark's territorial integrity or political independence.[219] Nazi Germany regarded Denmark as its model protectorate; Churchill called Denmark "Hitler's canary." Until August 1943, Denmark, unlike other occupied countries, continued largely to manage its own internal affairs, although it made many concessions to Nazi Germany, such as imposing censorship to suppress any open dissatisfaction with the occupying power. Basically, the arrangement was that under the occupation the Germans would control Danish territory, while the Danes would control their own society.[220]

Despite its policy of collaboration, the Danish government steadfastly refused to make three concessions to the Germans: first, the Danish army would not fight on the German side in the war; second, it would not impose capital punishment for sabotage or other crimes; and, third, it would not enact discriminatory laws against the Jews.[221] In the first years of the occupation, Germany acquiesced on these three issues. The Germans were satisfied with a status quo that allowed the Danes to govern themselves, and they did not give any support to an unsuccessful attempt by Danish Nazis in 1940 to seize power through a coup.

From April 1940 to August 1943, the local German authorities maintained a low profile and encouraged the government in Berlin to do the same, because Germany benefited from a peaceful Denmark.[222] Danish agriculture supplied Germany with a substantial proportion of its food needs, so the Germans had no desire to rock the boat.

Furthermore, because there were relatively few Jews in Denmark, the "Jewish issue" had only marginal significance from the Nazi perspective.[223]

One must keep in mind, however, that during the early years of the occupation the Germans left the Danish Jews alone only because the Danish government and public resisted every effort by the Germans to impose anti-Jewish laws or to take any action against the Jews. The Danes made it clear to the Germans that any attack on the Jews would trigger an uprising by the Danes, and the German occupiers had a strong interest in a pacific, stable Denmark.

During the first three and a half years of the occupation, the German occupation authorities periodically placed pressure on the Danish government to adopt anti-Semitic laws and restrictions. The government always resisted this pressure, saying that there was no "Jewish problem" in Denmark. Contrary to an enduring legend, King Christian X of Denmark never wore, or threatened to wear, the yellow star that Jews were forced to wear in other occupied countries, if only for the simple reason that no Jew in Denmark was ever compelled to wear the star.

The story about the king, however, although factually untrue, does contain a deeper truth: throughout the occupation, the king did provide strong moral support for Danish independence, including protection of the Jewish population. When Danish Nazis tried to set fire to the Copenhagen synagogue, the king sent his sympathies to the rabbi. Thus, the Danish state and government, while cooperating with the Nazi occupiers in many respects, steadfastly protected its Jewish population. No other occupied country acted in this way.

Technically, Denmark was neutral; it was neither at war

with Germany nor an ally of Germany. Its small army and navy remained under Danish command. The German Foreign Office continued to be the official link to Denmark, although the German ambassador in Copenhagen was given the rank of "Plenipotentiary." There was even a free election in Denmark in March 1943 (the only one held in any country occupied by Germany), in which 96 percent of the electorate supported the four democratic political parties, rather than the Danish Nazi party.

During the first years of the occupation, Harald and Else and their daughter Lilian continued to live their lives fairly normally in Charlottenlund, a suburb of Copenhagen. Harald kept his post as the Medalist of the Royal Danish Mint. According to Harald:

> The conditions were bearable in Denmark during the initial years [of the occupation], but we were always under a nerve-wrecking [sic] pressure, since we never knew what would happen. Hence, [the German decision to deport the Jews in October 1943] didn't hit us unexpectedly, as much as we kept hoping that they wouldn't have enough time before they were themselves vanquished.

And Max's wife, Nora, writing from Sweden in November 1942 about the dangerous situation that her mother-in-law, Johanna Salomon, faced in occupied Norway, added that "even Harald [in Denmark] is living on a volcano." Nonetheless, despite the anxiety that the occupation created, their everyday lives continued on a fairly normal basis. They continued to take their vacations, and on at least one occasion took a bicycle trip to visit Alfred in a mental hospital in the city of Roskilde, about thirty miles away.

There was little Danish resistance during the first three years of the German occupation. Beginning in 1942-43, however, an underground resistance movement, led by Communists, committed acts of sabotage, which the Danish government discouraged but was powerless to stop. During the summer of 1943, acts of sabotage and a wave of strikes provoked Werner Best, the German plenipotentiary, to demand that the Danish government take action to suppress the resistance, including the imposition of the death penalty for sabotage. The government rejected Best's demands; and on August 29, 1943, Best imposed martial law. The Danish elected government resigned, although the administrative offices of the government continued to operate. The Danish Navy scuttled its ships to prevent them from falling into the hands of the Germans, and the Germans interned the small Danish Army. The king was placed under house arrest in his Copenhagen palace.

The government's resignation in August removed the protection Denmark's Jews had enjoyed, and on September 8 Best requested permission from Hitler to deport them for the purpose of exterminating them. Hitler quickly gave permission, and a Gestapo detachment and a ship were sent to Copenhagen to arrest the Jews and carry them to Germany and death in one of the extermination camps. The arrests were to occur during the night of October 1 and into the early hours of October 2.

Having set in motion the action against the Jews, Best was at the very least half-hearted in its execution and perhaps worked actively to sabotage it. Although Best was a hard-core Nazi and an anti-Semite, his interest seems to have been to banish the Danish Jews, not to kill them. Moreover, Best was in the midst of a three-way bureaucratic struggle among the German Foreign Office, the Wehrmacht, and the Gestapo over which would have ultimate authority in Denmark. Best, who as plenipotentiary worked for Ribbentrop's Foreign Office, could consolidate his own power only by keeping Denmark peaceful. This was best achieved by expelling the Danish Jews as quickly and quietly as possible. He knew that a forcible roundup and deportation of the Jewish Danes would trigger strikes and disturbances throughout the country.

Thus, Best had a selfish interest in facilitating the escape of the Danish Jews. To the Danes, Best could truthfully claim that he had helped save the Jews; to the Germans he could claim with equal truth that he had rid the country of the Jews. Furthermore, his actions might enable him to avoid responsibility for the murder of the Danish Jews after an Allied victory, which appeared increasingly likely in late 1943.

Best therefore seems to have done his best to enable the escape to take place. He instructed the police making the roundups of Jews not to break into houses and apartments, but to leave if nobody answered their knock. Not a single one of the boats transporting the Jews to Sweden was intercepted by the German navy. According to Kirchhoff, "the obstruction and passivity shown by the plenipotentiary and the occupation authorities were crucial for the outcome that the Holocaust took a different course in Denmark from elsewhere in Hitler's Europe."[224]

The apparent complicity of the Germans in the escape in no way detracts from the united support Danish Jews received from the Danish people, the heroism of Danish rescuers, or the genuine fear felt by Jewish escapees; at the time, they had no way of knowing whether the Germans would attack Danish Jews with the same single-minded ruthlessness they had demonstrated in every other one of the occupied countries.

Most important for the success of the escape, on September 28 Best's aide, George Duckwitz, leaked the date of the roundup to members of the Danish Social Democratic Party. Historians of the Danish rescue believe that it is unlikely Duckwitz would have taken this step without Best's authorization.[225] The information was conveyed to leaders of the Jewish community and to Acting Rabbi Dr. Marcus Melchior of Copenhagen's Krystalgade Synagogue. Melchior appeared in street clothes before the members of his congregation on the morning of September 29, the day of the beginning of Rosh Hashonah (the Jewish New Year), and told them that the New Year's services would not be held that evening. Instead, he warned, all Jews should go into hiding or flee the country.[226]

The German action against the Jews began at 9:30 p.m. on October 1, but by that time most of Denmark's Jews had gone underground. Non-Jewish Danes hid the Jews and helped them escape in fishing boats across the Øresund, the strait that separates Denmark from Sweden. The Øresund is about twenty-five miles wide at its widest point. At a latitude of about 56 degrees, the water is cold and often rough in October.

Of Denmark's 8,000 Jews, about 7,300 escaped. Four hundred and eighty-one were arrested in Denmark and sent to the Theresienstadt concentration camp in Czechoslovakia.[227] Among these were leaders of the Jewish community whom the Germans had taken hostage, including

Rabbi Melchior, and the defenseless occupants of a Jewish old-age home next to the Copenhagen synagogue, who were brutally treated by the Germans. No Danish Jews, however, were sent to the extermination camps. The Danish civil authorities continued to take an interest in them while they were prisoners at Theresienstadt, sent them food, and on one occasion visited the camp. The total death toll of Danish Jews, including those who drowned while escaping or committed suicide, was 116.

The rescue operation was organized not by the Danish resistance movement but by a broad spectrum of Danish society. In the streets of Copenhagen, people who were total strangers went up to Jews and offered them the keys to their apartments. A woman in a suburban train, overhearing a conversation between two persons involved in the rescue work, came up to them and gave them all the cash in her handbag.[228] Networks of rescuers were hastily organized by doctors and other groups. Jews were hidden in Copenhagen's hospitals until they could safely be transported to Sweden.[229] The Danish police cooperated with the rescuers, to the point of arresting a man who had taken money from them by falsely claiming that the money was for the rescue operation. It is estimated that between 30,000 and 40,000 Danes participated in the rescue operation, and many others assisted simply by remaining silent. As one rescuer said, "In those days everything was possible when it was a question of helping the persecuted Jews."[230] In contrast to other occupied countries, there were very few instances of Danes denouncing Jews to the Germans.

The fishermen who transported the Jews to Sweden were well paid for their services. In the first days of the rescue, there were instances of gouging and extortion, with several thousand kroner being paid. Harald Salomon paid 3,500 kroner to the fisherman who took him, Else, and Lilian over on October 2; and he paid the very large sum of 5,000 kroner to take Johanna two days later.[231] After a short time, the going rate was set at 500 kroner per person, with a discount for large groups. On the night of October 8 and during the early hours of October 9, a boat took 230 passengers to Sweden for 100,000 kroner, or 434 kroner per person. In general, neither the rescuers nor the rescued begrudged the profits made by the persons who manned the boats, since they were risking the loss of their boats and their livelihood if they were caught, not to speak of their freedom and their lives.[232]

Escape to Sweden had been possible before October 1943, although few people attempted it. The Danish authorities had advised the Jews not to try to escape, for fear that it would arouse German suspicions and provoke them to attack the Jewish population. Furthermore, in the early days of the war Sweden was unwilling to arouse German hostility by accepting large numbers of Jewish refugees. Before the Germans declared martial law in Denmark on August 29, about 100 persons a month crossed over. In September, 600 made the crossing, most of them Danish soldiers and sailors who planned to join the Allied forces in England.

The escape began during the first days of October and reached its zenith on October 8 and 9, when about 2,500 persons made the crossing. By October 21, the evacuation was substantially complete, although a few hundred people reached Sweden during the ensuing two months. In all, over 7,000 Jews escaped in 600 to 700 crossings, many in small boats, from more than fifty embarkation points.[233]

Site where the Danish Brigade crossed to Denmark, May 6, 1945

Coast Road, route of the Danish Brigade to Copenhagen

Helsingør (Elsinore)

Helsingborg

SWEDEN

ØRESUND

DENMARK

Copenhagen

Escape route of Harald, Else, and Lilian, October 1–2, 1943

Malmö

Why did the Danes, unlike the populations of other occupied countries such as Norway, France, and Poland, unite to help their Jewish compatriots escape German annihilation? This question has occupied the attention of many historians of Denmark and the Holocaust. Yahil lists five factors that contributed to the success of the Danish rescue: (1) the small number of Jews in Denmark; (2) the special political conditions prevailing in the "model protectorate" of Denmark; (3) the geographical proximity of neutral Sweden; (4) the fact that the rescue took place in 1943, after the war had turned in favor of the Allies; and (5) "the special character and moral stature of the Danish people and their love of democracy and freedom."[234] According to Yahil, the last of these factors—the character of the people—brought the other factors together and was crucial in making the rescue possible. Norway, for example, had a much smaller Jewish population than Denmark and was equally close to Sweden, but more than one-third of the Jews living in Norway in 1940 were killed in the Holocaust.

To understand the special nature of Danish democracy, one has to go back to the mid nineteenth century, when the cultural historian, theologian, and poet N.F.S Grundtvig organized a new system of education, based on folk high schools.[235] The aim of these schools was not so much to teach knowledge as to develop the minds of the pupils along democratic and humanistic lines. "Lectures, singing, conversation, physical exercises, history, folk-lore [were] the characteristic features of these highly original foundations."[236] Danish culture came to equate national patriotism with deeply felt values of equality and democracy. The Danish Lutheran Church viewed Jews and Christians as members of a common religious family.[237] Danish agriculture, which was largely composed of small holdings as a result of nineteenth-century land reform, and the socialist labor movement combined to create a culture in which defense of the rights of the underprivileged was crucial to the moral order of society.[238] A description of the Danish character written in 1915 would have been equally applicable in 1943:

> The national characteristics of the Danish people are generosity; slowness of speech; a good-humour which has become proverbial; determination almost amounting to truculence, especially in the case of peasants; an immense capacity for hard work and sustained effort; extreme democratic principles; a strange fatalism which is a mixture of scepticism and hesitation; and finally, a complete and wonderful fearlessness in throwing over traditions and prejudices.
>
> Their dreams are of a very practical nature, and there is about them a certain atmosphere of clean and sane humanitarianism which is very attractive. They seem to carry out their reforms in a spirit of common sense which is almost scientific. Perhaps this is because their temperament is genuinely, rather than sentimentally, democratic.[239]

The relevance of Grundtvik's teachings to the Danes in 1940 is made clear by the fact that, during the early days of the German occupation, a Danish theology professor named Hal Koch gave fiery public lectures on Grundtvik to huge enthusiastic audiences, aimed at bringing about national unity and reinforcement of the nation's democratic ideals in a time of great crisis. Koch vigorously opposed the anti-Jewish legislation that Germany was trying to force on the Danish government.[240]

As far back as the eighteenth century, the Danish monarchy encouraged integration of Jews into Danish society. In 1788, Jews were permitted to join craft guilds in Copenhagen, and ten years later they were permitted to study at the university and other institutions of higher learning.[241] Nevertheless, Denmark was not immune to the virus of anti-Semitism. In 1813, a great deal of anti-Semitic propaganda circulated in Denmark, accusing the Jews of causing the country's bankruptcy that year, which was more likely the result of its disastrous participation in the Napoleonic Wars; and in 1819 there was a pogrom in Copenhagen, which was witnessed by Hans Christian Andersen, who had just arrived in Copenhagen from the Danish provinces as a fourteen-year-old, when Jewish shops were destroyed and Jews were attacked on the streets.[242] This, however, was the last major anti-Jewish demonstration ever to take place in Denmark.

By the middle of nineteenth century, there was little room for anti-Semitism in the egalitarian Danish society. The authors of a description of Danish life, written in 1915, mentions the country's Jewish population without singling them out for comment; they stated dispassionately: "There are only 4,500 Roman Catholics in Denmark, and about the same number of Jews."[243] The same book describes Georg Brandes, who was then a famous literary critic, as "perhaps the greatest living Dane and one of the most potent forces in European letters of the day," but never once mentions the fact that Brandes was Jewish.[244]

Like Georg Brandes before him, Harald Salomon was first and foremost a Dane, and he was highly respected as an artist both in Denmark and abroad. The fact of his Jewish background was irrelevant to his life, except of course in the eyes of the Nazis.

After the Nazis occupied Denmark, whatever anti-Semitism existed in the country disappeared almost entirely. The safety of the Jews became a matter of concern, not just to Danish officialdom but to the Danish public generally.[245] After three years of occupation by Germany and Danish concessions to many German demands, many Danes felt that the moral order that they treasured had deteriorated. When the Germans threatened to deport the Jews, the Danes united to save them not because they were Jews, but because the Danes felt that by victimizing the Jews the Germans were attacking the fundamental values of Danish society.[246] It was almost universally accepted in Denmark at the time that preserving democracy was essential to the survival of the country.[247] A leader of one of the groups that organized the rescue put this idea very clearly: "It was not only the Jews who were threatened by destruction by the Nazis. It was our very civilization, the moment we surrendered our Jews to their pursuers."[248]

The rescue operation could not have succeeded without the willingness of Sweden to accept the refugees. By August 1943, two key events had transformed Swedish refugee policy from its prewar policy of resisting the entry of Jews fleeing Hitler to one of generosity and welcome. First, the Swedish government was aware of Germany's Final Solution; the brutal German deportation of over 700 Norwegian Jews to extermination camps the previous winter had been broadcast throughout Sweden by the clergy and the press, arousing enormous indignation and horror. By October 1943, Swedish public opinion was ready to back any government decisions favoring Jewish refugees. Secondly, with an Allied victory in sight, Swedish policy-makers saw that humanitarian efforts would help Sweden to atone for its pro-German stance earlier in the war and avoid the displeasure of the United Nations and the other Scandinavian countries. Thus, genuine altruism and calculating *realpolitik* combined to shape Swedish policy in favor of helping the Danish Jews.[249]

Within two days after martial law was declared on August 29, the Swedish foreign ministry concluded that it was only a matter of time before the Germans would act against the Danish Jews and Sweden would be called upon to respond. By August 31, Sweden was prepared to grant entry visas to Jews who could claim Swedish citizenship, and it appears that the Swedish legation in Copenhagen was willing to grant Swedish citizenship on a liberal basis to any Danish Jew wishing to enter Sweden. It was not so clear, however, that the German authorities in Denmark would grant exit visas to these newly minted Swedes. By September 14, the Swedish government had decided to accept all Danish Jews, with or without visas;[250] and by the third week of September — over a week before the Danish rescue began — the government had prepared an old castle in southern Sweden for use as a Danish refugee center.[251]

The situation became critical on Wednesday, September 29, when the Swedish ambassador in Copenhagen cabled his government that "according to trustworthy information, it is expected that on Friday or Saturday morning 6,000 Jews are expected to be taken away and sent by boat to Germany." The government immediately cabled Arvid

Richert, its minister in Berlin, suggesting to him that he make sure the Germans understood the "extraordinary indignation such measures will bring about in Sweden and offering to take charge of the Jews and intern them in Sweden for the rest of the war."[252] Richert, who did not believe that there was anything that Sweden could do to stop the imminent deportation of the Danish Jews, cabled back that he had inquired and had been told that the rumors of a deportation of the Danish Jews were without foundation.

Neither the Swedish foreign ministry nor the Swedish ambassador in Denmark believed the Germans' denial. At noon on October 1, Richert was instructed to make a formal offer to the German government that Sweden would accept and to intern the Danish Jews.[253] Richert made the offer, to which the Germans did not reply. Sweden decided to act anyway. At 7:00 p.m. the next day, October 2, a representative of the Swedish Foreign Ministry made a radio broadcast from Stockholm, extending an offer from the Swedish government to accept all the Danish Jews.[254]

It was the first time any western government had agreed publicly to give unconditional asylum to refugees from Nazi Germany. This decision had enormous practical consequences. Now captains of fishing boats and other vessels carrying the Danish Jews could enter Swedish waters and ports without fear of being intercepted or having their boats interned. It was a gesture of Scandinavian solidarity and a rebuke to the Nazi leaders, and it went unchallenged by the German government. It demonstrated that, at least under the special circumstances that prevailed at that time and place, the Holocaust could be resisted.

The escape from Denmark of Harald, Else, and Lilian

most likely occurred on the night of October 1, one day before the historic Swedish announcement. Ironically, Harald's prominence and his acquaintance with persons who had good access to information probably made his escape more onerous than of a person of less privileged status. It is likely that he learned of the impending arrest of the Danish Jews earlier than did most Danish Jews, perhaps before Rabbi Melchior's announcement to his congregation on September 29.

It seems certain that Harald and his family fled before the evening of October 2, when the Swedish government publicly announced its willingness to accept the Jews. Since the Swedish position had not yet been made clear to the rescuers or the refugees, the fishermen who took them across the Øresund were unwilling to take their boat into a Swedish port for fear that the Swedish government would intern them and the boat.

As a result, Harald, Else, and Lilian were forced to leave the boat before it reached shore and to swim the last part of their journey in the cold October waters of the Øresund. In this respect, their experience is unique in the published accounts of the Danish rescue. If they had sailed even one day later, they would have disembarked comfortably in a Swedish port, as did almost every other person who escaped, including Harald's mother, Johanna a few days later. After October 2, the Swedish government ordered its navy to keep all German warships out of Swedish waters, and the Swedes even facilitated the rescue by providing fuel to the fishermen carrying the refugees.[255]

Here is how Harald and his family escaped. A fellow official at the Royal Danish Mint tipped Harald off about the German decision to arrest and deport the Jews and advised him and his family to go into hiding immediately. Harald was married to a non-Jew, so the arrest order would not apply to him, but it is not clear that Harald knew this.[256] Even if he had known, he had no assurance that the Germans would not extend the arrests to persons in his situation. In the event, Harald, Else, and Lilian went into hiding in the home of Danish Christian friends, who arranged with a fisherman to take them across the Øresund to Sweden.

Because the Germans had imposed a 9:00 p.m. curfew, Harald, Else, and Lilian left their friends' home before nightfall and hid in a shack on the beach at Skovshoved, a few miles up the coast from Copenhagen, where the fisherman kept his equipment. On the way there, they met a Danish policeman, who asked Harald what he was doing out with his family. Harald replied: "You know very well what I am doing. I hope that you are going to be a loyal Dane." The policeman let them go.

They waited all night among the fishing gear, but the fisherman did not show up. A member of the rescue organization led them to another shack, at a place called Frihavn, near the Copenhagen suburb of Hellerup. Harald insisted to their Danish guide that he padlock the door from the outside. When asked why, he replied so that no one would suspect that there was anyone inside. Actually, a German patrol did come around, but left when they saw that the shack was padlocked. Harald's precaution was wise: there are reports that others who hid in boat sheds were discovered by the Germans and dragged off as prisoners, and that those who tried to flee were hunted down.[257]

Eventually, at 6:00 in the morning, the fisherman who had agreed to take them arrived, and they boarded his small boat. The three were the only passengers. They all were hidden in the bottom of the boat, but Lilian, who was ten years old at the time, remembers that someone, perhaps a Danish policeman, came on board, peered into the hold, and noticed Lilian's long hair. But when he saw Lilian, he said it was not a problem since she was only a child.He left without making any further inspection of the boat or its cargo.

They had been at sea for about two hours when the fisherman told them he would go no further. In the mist, they could not see land. They were about 500 meters from the shore at Lommabukten, a wide bay a few miles north of Malmö, the Swedish city directly across the Øresund from Copenhagen. The fisherman told them to get out of the boat and swim to land. First, Harald stripped to his underwear, climbed down and took Lilian ashore, and then he returned for Else. The fisherman threw their suitcase into the sea. As they waded in, they saw a farmer plowing a field with a horse. He must have been quite surprised, seeing no boat, just three people emerging from the sea.

Harald described their escape in a letter written to Gerda a few weeks later. Parts of the letter, including the day and month it was written, were clipped out by a censor (presumably either Swedish or American):

> I am finally getting it together to write you a letter.
> As Mother told you, we had to flee from home. I
> managed to rescue Mother from the grip of the
> assassins once, but the second time was a close call.
> The rumors that the Danish Jews were next kept
> growing stronger, and we finally had to decide to
> escape, we all tried to get away [censored] and due to

the curfew banning use of the streets after 9 p.m., we all had to hide in a tiny shack where we sat all night long. It was neither pleasant nor fun.

Later on, we had to hide in the homes of friends, until [censored]. Then Else, Lilian and I spent yet another night in a shack. At 6.a.m., we made it out of the harbor despite the surveillance of the Germans. It was a game of chance with our lives at stake, but we succeeded. Mother was unable to come along since we had to swim ashore in Sweden. Luckily, Mother made it here. [censored] It if weren't for all of our good friends who helped us along, I am sure it would never have worked, but we have now seen proof that we have many friends who really made an effort to rescue us.

When we arrived at the coast of Sweden, we had to jump into the water more than 500 meters from shore and swim. I put Lilian in a lifesaver, and after we had swum for a while, we were able to reach the bottom and wade ashore, where we found a tiny farm where I had to leave Lilian behind. Then I had to jump back into the water to get Else, who had not managed to [censored] get back onboard again. Then Else had to stand on the deck in the freezing cold for more than half an hour. Finally, the fisherman took off his clothes and swam with her so I could meet her halfway, but at that point, she was more dead than alive. Thank God [censored] strength.

We got ashore [censored] fully soaked.

Harald's mother, Johanna, also described Harald's escape in a letter written from Jönköping, Sweden, on October 8:

> Harald, Else, and Lilian had a terrible crossing. The captain did not want to risk anything and left them on a sandbank off the Swedish coast. Then Harald had to rescue himself, Else and Lilian. They all had to take their clothes off, and got ashore in a desolate place dressed only in their underwear. The waves were high and it was bitterly cold. [Harald] was in the water for an hour, and when he finally got ashore, he was so battered and exhausted that people thought he was 50 years old [he was actually 43].

On the journey they lost all their clothes, including those they had been wearing. The farmer who took them in gave them dry garments. He then called the police, who asked Harald if he knew anyone in Sweden. Harald mentioned a man he had once worked with. The police called the man and told him to take in the three Danish escapees. They stayed in the man's home for about two weeks, his wife being none too gracious about having uninvited guests.

Johanna did not escape to Sweden with Harald and his family because she was told in advance that she would have to swim or wade ashore and, at the age of seventy-two, she felt she could not. When Harald and his family went into hiding with his friends in Copenhagen, she went with them, but Harald was forced to leave without her. Harald was reluctant, but his friends assured him they would get her to Sweden. They arranged for her to be hidden in a hospital for two and a half days. By that date, October 4, the Danes had organized the rescue and had established procedures for the hiding of the Danish Jews and transporting them to Sweden.[259]

When Johanna left the hospital, she was not allowed to take any luggage; it had to look as if she was taking a short rail trip. After the rescue, she wrote to Gerda in New York: "Once more, we have now lost *everything* we had. I have nothing but the dress, the coat, and the shoes I am wearing. My last little suitcase containing the most essential items was left behind at the hospital, but after all, we did save our own lives!" All she could bring with her was 4,000 kroner. She escaped on a small motorboat on October 4 with seven other women whom she did not know. She and the other passengers hid in the bottom of the boat underneath a crate of fish, with a bucket for seasickness, as the sea was very rough. They arrived completely exhausted in Sweden, where Swedish soldiers welcomed them and helped them ashore.

Johanna was taken by bus to the town of Ramlösa, near Helsingborg, which was used as a gathering point for the refugees. After spending two days recuperating there, she got in touch with her son and daughter-in law, Max and Nora, who were then living in the south Swedish city of Jönköping, and she joined them there on October 7. Nora wrote: She is staying with us for now, but it gets crowded with 6 people sharing 2 rooms and kitchen."[260]

Recalling that time (or more likely recalling what her parents later told her about it), Max's older daughter Frøydis says that Johanna drove Nora nuts. Johanna was anxious to help with household chores, and she took on all of the family's darning and mending work. However, she could never get along with any of her daughters-in-law, and she soon moved to a rented room. Until she returned to Denmark at the end of the war eighteen months later, she lived alone near her son's house and went over for dinner there every evening.

The rescue from Denmark was not inexpensive. Besides the 8,500 kroner that Harald had to pay the fishermen for the two rescue trips, they lost all their clothes and had to purchase necessary items when they arrived in Sweden. Harald estimated that the rescue cost him 10 to 12,000 Danish kroner (at least $60,000 in 2004 dollars). When they arrived, they were in a straitened financial condition. Also, Harald suffered from back pain and other ailments (which he described as sciatica) for several months as a result of his one-hour exposure and exhausting experience in the chilly October sea.

Because he was well known as a coin designer and sculptor, within less than a week after his escape Harald received several job offers from Swedish firms, including one from a large jewelry firm in Stockholm. He accepted an offer from the Rörstrand Porcelain Factory in the small town of Lidköping, which he described as the best porcelain factory in Sweden, and went to work designing figurines and decorating vases and other objects with reliefs. This was a kind of work that he had never done before, and it enabled him to learn new techniques and broaden his artistic ability.

His pay was modest; at first, 450 Swedish kroner a month (about $2,500 in 2004 dollars). The porcelain pieces he designed sold well, and in February 1945 there was an exhibition of them in Stockholm, which was favorably reviewed by the newspapers. After the war, he continued to do work at the Rörstrand factory during his six-week summer vacations, in order to augment his government salary. During his exile in Sweden, he also sculpted a bust of Lilian, which he thought was the best thing he ever made.

They lived in Lidköping for about eighteen months. At first the three of them slept and ate in a single room; but later they moved into a tiny, partially furnished apartment. Lilian was happy to go back to school, and not much later she managed to write the best essay in her class (in Swedish).

Although his situation was far better than that of most of the Danish refugees in Sweden, Harald felt powerless and frustrated while in exile. He wrote later: "We had our daily work, we lived in safety and we stood outside the battle against the oppressors."[261] In 1944, a military unit called the Danish Brigade was organized by Danish exiles in Sweden for the purpose of participating in the liberation of Denmark from the Germans. Harald volunteered to join in August 1944, but he was rejected because of his age. He was forty-four, and the maximum age was thirty-five. However, in February 1945 he learned that a Drivers' Corps was being formed that accepted older men. He joined the corps on April 3, 1945, and was given a rigorous three-week training course for military drivers, which included night driving under difficult conditions, automobile mechanics, signaling, map reading, and the handling of firearms and explosives. Max, whom Harald visited in Jönköping on his way home after completing his training, wrote to Gerda on April 29: "The training has done him good, he looked sunburnt and much better than for years. He must keep himself ready for service on call."

The call came almost immediately. The German forces in Denmark surrendered on May 4, and that night the 5,000 men of the Brigade gathered in Helsingborg. On the morning of May 6, the Brigade, including Harald's unit, crossed the narrow straits between Helsingborg in Sweden to Helsingor (Elsinore) in Denmark on ferries and naval minesweeepers, not knowing whether or not there would be a fight with the Germans when they arrived. On the same day, the first British troops reached Copenhagen. This is how Harald told the story:

> By that time, it was Sunday afternoon on May 6, and around 1 p.m. we started on the [30-mile] journey to Copenhagen that none of us will ever forget. Along the entire Strandvejen [Beach Road], people were lined up to greet the Brigade. It was lovely to feel their warmth streaming towards us. I must admit that we did honk our horns quite a bit during the trip. Occasionally, we saw the familiar face of a friend or family member. Some just happened to be out on a Sunday stroll in the beautiful, sunny weather, others knew that the Brigade was on its way and had figured it was likely that some of their acquaintances in Sweden would return home as Danish soldiers.[262]

The joyous atmosphere of the march to Copenhagen abruptly ended when they reached the city. At an intersection, snipers opened fire with automatic weapons on the Brigade and the spectators from windows and roofs of the buildings. Apparently, not all the German soldiers in Denmark had surrendered. The fire might also have come from members of the Hipo, the Danish Nazi militia.

During the first days of the liberation, the Resistance Movement, bent on revenge after the five years of the occupation, was hunting down these people, as well as informers and other collaborators.[263] Harald reported on the firefight:

> Panic immediately broke loose among the many spectators, who instantly understood that they were risking their lives just as the war had come to an end, at a time when peace and order were supposed to be restored in Copenhagen. We darted out of our vehicles and took our positions where we could find cover from the gunfire coming from the rooftops. We fired at the windows and buildings from where the bullets came. With great admiration, we watched the ambulance personnel, who ran back and forth in the crossfire searching for injured people in need of help.

The firing lasted three-quarters of an hour[264] (Harald recalled that it lasted a few hours), and several people were killed and wounded. When it ended, the Brigade continued its march and reached central Copenhagen, where Harald's unit was housed in a public school. In true Danish fashion, the Women's Voluntary Service "welcomed us with generous rations of butter and cheese." After sixty-five hours without sleep, they got to bed at 2:00 on Monday morning.

VE Day, the day celebrating the end of the war against Germany, was May 8, Harald's forty-fifth birthday. He spent the day in transit with other units of the Brigade to southern Jutland, close to the German border. He wrote: "My greatest experience [there] was watching the Germans retreat southwards. It was a crestfallen master race that walked its way home, oftentimes in pouring rain for hours on end." A month later, Harald was discharged from the Brigade. Meanwhile, Else and Lilian had returned to Denmark. A picture taken at that time shows Harald in his Danish Brigade uniform, beaming with his delighted wife and daughter in front of their house. Shortly afterwards, he wrote:

> The great majority of us value the time we spent as military drivers for the Brigade from Sweden, and we will look back at it with joy, especially the wonderful camaraderie that quickly formed among the motley crew of drivers and soldiers.

By early July, Harald was back working at the Mint; his position had been kept open for him during his absence. The day before he escaped to Sweden, Harald had deeded his house to an acquaintance in order to prevent its confiscation by the Germans. The assignee and his family were living in the house on their return to Copenhagen, and they were reluctant to leave. By August, however, they had moved out; and Harald, Else, and Lilian were able to resume their previous lives.

Alfred in Denmark

———

{1940-1945}

AT THE TIME OF THE GERMAN INVASION, Alfred
had been a mental patient in Roskilde Hospital for six
months.

He was plagued by obsessive thoughts of persecution,
which in itself was not irrational, considering the time and
the circumstances. But it was not just that. He had halluci-
nations and engaged in irrational and harmful behavior. He
was diagnosed as suffering from acute psychosis. He was
discharged from the hospital in April 1941. By that time,
his wife Hjørdis and their three daughters, then aged fif-
teen, thirteen, and five, had moved in with Hjørdis's sister,
who was a widow with children of her own. Alfred's brother Harald, who apparently had been appointed guardian of
Alfred's assets, had sold the house Alfred and his family
had lived in. Furthermore, Hjørdis had decided to divorce
him.

After leaving the hospital, Alfred worked as a farm
laborer for a few months, but he did not keep the job for
long. Without a family or a home, he moved in with
Harald, but the two brothers did not get along well togeth-

er. To make matters worse, Else's brother, who also suffered from mental illness, likewise wanted to live at Harald's. For a while, there was even some discussion, crazy as it may sound to us now, of Alfred leaving the comparative safety of Denmark and moving to occupied Norway to stay with Johanna. Fortunately for him, he was unable to obtain a visa from the Nazi authorities in Norway. Meanwhile, his behavior became erratic, and he wasted the little money that he had on women and liquor.

In January 1942, Alfred was hospitalized again. Until October 1943, when Harald fled Denmark with his family, he had visited Alfred from time to time in the hospital and consulted with the doctors about Alfred's treatment. After Harald managed to escape from Denmark and had gone to live with his family in Sweden, Alfred's care (and his fate) rested solely in the hands of the hospital staff.

Despite the German attempt to deport the Danish Jews in October 1943, Alfred was not discovered or harmed.

It is a marvelous testimony to the Danish national character that throughout the period that Alfred was hospitalized and certainly not able to protect himself, no administrator, doctor, nurse, or orderly at the hospital informed the Germans of the presence of a Jewish patient in the hospital.[265]

Although Alfred seemed to have recovered from the worst of his illness by early 1945, the hospital's medical and administrative staff kept him within its sheltering walls as a patient in order to protect him from deportation to Germany.

Even after the Liberation in May 1945, Alfred Salomon continued to be fearful of the Nazis. Plans for him to leave the hospital in June were therefore postponed, and he was not finally discharged from the hospital until four months later, in October 1945.

Grete and Joe.

The Life and Death of Grete

{1901-1954}

GRETE SALOMON did not share in the wartime experiences of her mother Johanna, her brothers Harald, Max, and Alfred, and sister Gerda. Nevertheless, she was always closely connected to them, and throughout her life thought of herself as Norwegian.

Grete was born on August 30, 1901, and grew up in Oslo. She lost her father at fourteen. At sixteen she became engaged, but Johanna, no doubt wisely, quickly put an end to it. In order to prepare Grete for married life, Johanna sent her to a cooking school in Copenhagen, where she studied for two years. Throughout her life, Grete was an excellent cook and pastry chef. Her masterpiece, much loved by her children, was a chocolate cake topped by large spheres of chocolate buttercream.

In 1919, the summer she turned eighteen, Grete met Jack Poser[266] at the Danish seaside resort of Hornbæk, which was frequented by upper-middle class Jewish families. Jack was born on February 23, 1892, in the Polish city of Cracow, then part of the Austro-Hungarian empire. He was the fourth of six sons of Isaac Poser, a wealthy Jewish fur dealer. Isaac's first wife had died after giving birth to the first three sons; Jack was the oldest son of Isaac and his second wife, Pauline. All six sons joined their father in the fur trade. After attending a business school in Berlin, Jack spent a year in New York when he was twenty, learning both the English language and the fur trade. Soon after returning to Europe, he joined his half-brother Siegfried (Sigi) in Denmark in order to avoid serving in the Austrian Army in the First World War. Jack worked as a fur dealer in Denmark and Sweden during the war.

Jack may have married Grete only because her older sister Gerda turned him away. He had first tried to court Gerda, but she preferred a certain Norwegian man. She told Jack he should "try" Grete instead. Johanna approved of Jack; he was a businessman and, even more important, Jewish. Grete wasn't sure whether she wanted to marry Jack; she was pitifully unsure of herself. But, like her mother, she probably felt he was a "good catch." After a short period of indecision, she agreed to marry him. Grete was eighteen; Jack was twenty-seven. After a two-year engagement, they were married on September 20, 1921, in Copenhagen. Probably because few of Jack's friends and family spoke Danish, the wedding invitations were printed in German. Gerda, whose first marriage was then ending, was prevented by her husband from leaving Berlin in time to take a train to Copenhagen, so she flew there in a chartered airplane, sitting in an open cockpit behind the pilot. According to a family story, they crash-landed in a field – without suffering any injury. Whether or not that story is true, she arrived in Copenhagen in time to see her sister get married.

It is understandable why Johanna approved of Jack as a suitable husband for her younger daughter. He had many excellent qualities. He was a hardworking, honest, practical businessman. Raised in a turbulent male-dominated Cracow household, he had a strong sense of family loyalty to his brothers. Unfortunately, he had other, less attractive characteristics. Although he could be generous, he was also controlling toward his family and insensitive to others. If Grete or one of the children disagreed with him, he would often retreat, maddeningly, into passive-aggressive silence. He had a persistent tendency to belittle those closest to him, which probably masked a deep insecurity. He and Grete were not a good match. Grete needed a stronger and more loving man who could reach out and care for her; Jack needed a stronger and more emotionally secure woman, who could stand up to him when necessary.

Shortly after the wedding, Grete and Jack moved to London, where Jack established a business in the City, London's financial district, as an agent for fur dealers in Leipzig, then the world center of the fur business, and later as an importer and exporter of furs. At first they lived at the Strand Palace, a large commercial hotel conveniently near the City. Grete complained that the hotel had bedbugs, but, far worse, she was left alone every day — friendless and cooped up in a hotel room in a strange city — while Jack worked long hours.

Soon afterwards the couple moved into a house on Dartmouth Road, a quiet street in Willesden, on the northwestern edge of London, that Johanna bought for them as a wedding present. The house cost £1,200 (perhaps about $200,000 in 2006 terms). This was the home where Jack and Grete and their children lived from 1922 until 1937, when the family moved to a somewhat larger new house near Finchley Road and Golders Green. In October

1922, they had a son, named Stephen, who died in infancy. Grete had medical problems at about this time, perhaps brought on by a miscarriage. Jack was greatly vexed, not from sympathy, but because the house had two floors, and he had climb the stairs to bring meals to her bedroom. Much later, when he gave his daughter, Liz, and her husband, Nat Gribin, a house in Great Neck, Long Island, he insisted that it have only one floor because of his distasteful memory of trotting up and down stairs to serve his sick wife.

Joe was born in 1924. He was named after Jack's eldest brother, who had died the previous year. As a child, Joe had bronchitis, so when he was five he was sent to Norway for several months, where Johanna took care of him. I was born in 1928. In 1932, the entire family summered in Norway. Johanna, Gerda, and Max and his dog Leo were living there; and Harald and Else visited from Copenhagen. For our return to England, Grete, who was prone to seasickness, decided to avoid the overnight ship across the rough North Sea from Bergen in Norway to Newcastle in England. Instead she traveled with me on a circuitous train ride through Sweden, Denmark, Germany, Belgium, and finally a short boat ride across the North Sea from Ostend to Harwich. Crossing the strait separating Sweden from Denmark, the train went right onto the ferry. At about midnight, we arrived at the Hamburg railway station, where we were met by a male friend who took us in a taxi to the hotel where we were to spend the night. Hamburg's bright lights and traffic were new and exciting to a four-year-old boy who had never before seen a big city at night. This was the last summer before Hitler came to power.

Jack and Grete lived a life of modest luxury in England. They became enthusiastic golfers. There is a photograph of Grete in the family album captioned in Jack's printed handwriting: "Westgate 1931. Playing in bogey!" (In England, bogey is the word for par.) She is slim, elegantly but simply dressed, wearing a beret at a jaunty angle, smiling at the camera, with a golf bag slung over her shoulder. Sometimes she played tennis on a private court near our home. For a while she took French lessons. She sometimes played the piano: classical music, including Chopin and

Grete golfing, Westgate-on-Sea, 1931.

Schubert; popular songs of the time, including music from the Fred Astaire movies; and nursery rhymes, such as "The Nutmeg Tree." I remember sitting as a small boy under the grand piano in the living room listening to her play.

Most summers during the 1930s, Jack and Grete rented houses at Westgate-on-Sea, a pleasant and unpretentious seaside resort near Canterbury in southeastern England. Revisited in 2001 after sixty-three years, the place had scarcely changed. Modest two-story houses; a flat eighteen-hole golf course; a waterfront lined with old-fashioned boarding houses; a long seawall where the water was over six feet deep at high tide; beaches a quarter of a mile wide at low tide; a grassy area next to the beach to picnic, play cricket, and fly kites. Summers at Westgate were heaven. Our family also spent a month every winter in St. Moritz. Grete loved winter sports and, as one might guess from her Norwegian childhood, was an excellent skier and skater. Jack's business provided a comfortable living even during the Depression years. There were servants: a cook and a maid who lived in, a chauffeur. When Liz was born in 1934, a nanny joined the live-in staff.

There was, however, an absence of warmth and mutual support in the family, which neither Jack nor Grete was able to provide. Jack's word was law, and Grete was too insecure to provide a counterpoise to his emotional coldness. Generally, he worked long hours during the week and played golf on the weekends. There were family outings that were eagerly looked forward to, such as an annual visit to Chipperfield Common near London to pick blackberries, but they were infrequent.

When Liz was born, Joe, then just ten years of age, was sent to Downsend, a boarding school in Surrey. He still recalls that he was so homesick at first that he took his letters from home to a place where he could be alone because he knew he would cry as soon as he began reading. Why did Jack and Grete send Joe into exile? Although the house contained a large nursery on the second floor facing the street which could have been used as a bedroom, they said there wasn't enough room in the house. To Joe, it was a rejection that he still feels vividly at the age of eighty-one.

Jack could be full of bonhomie with friends, but for the most part he was controlling and cold toward his wife and children. Like many married couples, Jack and Grete had quarrels, sometimes loud and terrifying ones, but Jack's usual practice was to retreat into silence when he was displeased. Sometimes he simply left the dinner table in the middle of a meal. On the surface, Grete had a stable and rather luxurious life: nice clothes, good food, a comfortable home, plenty of travel, and a set of friends, most of whom were Jack's business associates and their wives. She was, however, a deeply unhappy woman.

Grete never liked England, where she felt herself an outsider. During the 1930s, Jack took her on business trips to New York every December, where they stayed at the Essex House overlooking Central Park. She began to imagine New York as a much more congenial place than London. Her delusion that she could escape her unhappiness by moving there seems to have coincided with increasing depression and thoughts of suicide. When her sister Gerda visited her in London in the late 1930s, Grete complained to her about her life and marriage. She told Gerda that she had bought (or possibly only thought about buying) a gun. When Gerda sensibly suggested divorce as preferable to suicide, Grete replied that she would sooner be dead than divorced. In the late afternoons, she spent long periods alone in her bedroom with the shades drawn.

Grete did not hide her self-destructive thoughts. Much later, when Joe returned from the war in the Pacific he brought with him a Japanese pistol as a souvenir. One sunny day in 1946 or 1947, Grete asked him where he kept it. He deflected her, saying he had put the pistol away, but afterwards took the precaution of removing its firing pin. Today, Joe regrets that he didn't tell our father about this conversation, but the truth is Jack would have minimized the incident rather than trying to find out the source of Grete's distress.

Today, Grete would almost certainly have received treatment for serious depression, and/or she might have dissolved her unhappy marriage; but in the 1930s and '40s she felt herself trapped. Anti-depressant drugs were not yet on the market; psychiatry was regarded in her circle as an unacceptable admission of mental illness, and, barring a complete breakdown, Jack would have treated with contempt her suggestion that she seek treatment; finally, she was too emotionally frail and economically insecure to consider divorce, which would have involved social humiliation and a total upheaval of her life.

Grete's bleakness and desperation intensified in the summer of 1938, when she and Jack went on vacation in Switzerland with Kevork Allalemdjian, a friend and business associate, and his wife, Ilse, who had become Grete's closest friend. Ilse, who was thought to be recovering from a "nervous breakdown," committed suicide by jumping off the train on the journey back to England. This no doubt contributed to Grete's deepening sadness and perhaps nurtured an idea that she might end her own life. In retrospect, it seems significant that Grete's favorite opera was *Tosca*, in which the heroine leaps to her death from the Castel Sant' Angelo in Rome.

The next year, Jack and Grete took another summer holiday in Switzerland, this time accompanied by the children. World War II began while we were there, and Jack decided that instead of returning to England we should seek visas to enter the United States. Joe and I spent a happy two months at the Ecole Nouvelle de la Suisse Romande in Chailly, a suburb of Lausanne, while our parents and Liz, then five years old, stayed at the Eden Hotel in nearby Montreux waiting for the visas to come through. In November 1939 we traveled to the United States via Italy, which was not yet at war. On the way, we visited the Milan Cathedral. We embarked on the Italian liner *Conti di Savoia* at Genoa. The itinerary was leisurely, with a stop at Naples for the better part of a day to allow passengers to visit the ruins of Pompeii. After passing through the Straits of Gibraltar, we arrived in New York on a clear, cold Thanksgiving Day.

During Grete's first winter in New York, the family lived on Manhattan's Upper West Side in an apartment hotel that had cooking facilities. After that we moved to a grand duplex apartment on Riverside Drive and 89th Street — the same building where Babe Ruth, then retired from baseball, lived. In the 1940s, the Upper West Side was a haven for refugees from Germany; it was said that you could walk on Broadway from 86th to 100th Street without hearing a word of English. The Éclair bakery and restaurant on 72nd Street tried to reproduce the atmosphere — and cuisine — of a Viennese café. But this was not Grete's world; she was still a Norwegian at heart. In order to find Norwegian delicacies such as dark bread, sausage, and fish cakes, she drove all the way to Bay Ridge in Brooklyn where there were Norwegian grocery stores.

To all appearances, Grete had an enviable life, far from Nazi-occupied Europe and blitzed Britain. She shopped on Fifth Avenue, gave and was invited to bridge parties, played golf at a Westchester country club, had a subscription to the opera, vacationed in Miami Beach in the winter, New Hampshire in the summer, and White Sulphur Springs, West Virginia, in the spring. But Grete's enjoyment of these advantages was severely limited by her undiagnosed chronic depression. In 1942, doctors in New York decided that she suffered from hyperthyroidism, and she had an operation to remove part of her thyroid, without beneficial results.

In the summer of 1940, Jack invited his brother Sigi's two younger daughters, Doris and Lilian, sixteen and twelve, to join the family in New York for the duration of the war. He told Grete about this only as the ship from England neared port. For years she complained about the extra burden, complaints that may seem unreasonable since Doris and Lilian had been sent to New York to escape the bombing of Britain and a possible German invasion, and Grete had servants to help her. Her real cause for complaint was that Jack never consulted her about important matters that concerned the family and affected her life, including the addition to their household of two teenage girls.

Grete's happy childhood in Norway was frequently in her thoughts. In 1937, when Johanna was ill, Grete flew from London to Oslo to see her, an adventurous and even dangerous journey in those days. After the war, she visited her mother and her brothers several times in Scandinavia. But her relationship with her siblings was not always harmonious. Aside from Alfred, Grete was psychologically the weakest and least mature of the brothers and sisters. She lacked Max's seriousness and intellect, Gerda's independence of character and cheerful ability to meet adversity, and Harald's serenity and artistic talent.

Although Grete was not mean-spirited, difficulties with her marriage and chronic depression may have made her overly absorbed with her own problems. Many references to her in Max's and Harald's letters to Gerda during the war combine gratitude for money, food packages and other gifts with resentment at Grete's apparent indifference to their very real problems. A lack of warmth toward Grete is clear in their letters. After the war, when Max needed fabric for a suit, or business advice, from Jack, he wrote to Gerda, not to Grete, asking *her* to intercede for him.

In June 1948, when I graduated from Harvard College, Grete and Jack chose not to attend the commencement exercises; Joe was the only family member present. Instead, Jack and Grete took an ocean liner to London, where Helga Poser, a niece on Jack's side of the family, was to be married later that month. Jack told Joe and me to take a plane to join them there, but he did not tell Grete we were coming. The transatlantic crossing during the early years of commercial air travel and was quite an adventure. We flew in a Lockheed Constellation to Gander in Newfoundland and from there directly to London, a trip of about sixteen hours.

After the wedding, Grete and I flew to Copenhagen. Johanna, who had recently entered an old-age home, wrote about it to a friend:

I had a great joy. My daughter, Mrs. Poser, came to visit me with her second son, Norman. She and Mr. Poser traveled on [the *Queen Mary*] to London for the wedding of a niece. Mrs. Poser was mighty surprised when both her sons appeared there on the wedding day. Their father allowed them to come to London by plane across the Atlantic. Norman, who is 20 years old and has graduated from the university with flying colors, got an additional reward from his father, in that he was allowed to accompany his mother to Copenhagen. At present, he is visiting his uncle [Max] in Nordstrand for a few days.

Aside from the seemingly obvious question (unasked by anyone at the time) of why Jack and Grete did not attend my graduation and then fly to London for the wedding (as Joe and I did), the letter raises several other questions. First, the fact that Johanna referred to her younger daughter as "Mrs. Poser" suggests that the difference in their financial circumstances had distanced her from her daughter. Second, if Johanna was correct, Joe's and my flight across the Atlantic came as a surprise to Grete; Jack didn't bother to inform her of it in advance. Finally, it is unclear why Jack's decision not to attend the graduation but to allow his sons to attend a cousin's wedding could be considered a "reward" and why enabling me to see my grandmother in Copenhagen was an additional reward.

The 1948 visit was my first time in Copenhagen, and I found the city enchanting. The June weather was perfect. We ate strawberries and cream in the Tivoli Gardens, and there was a family luncheon in a country restaurant at Klampenborg, where we rode through the woods in a horse-drawn carriage. Although there still were food short-ages, one ate better in Denmark than anywhere else in Europe. In fact, as early as 1945, the Danes were sending food to the needy in other countries. Later, I took the overnight boat to Oslo, where I spent a week with Max, Nora, and their three children, Frøydis, Birgit, and Robert. There still were severe shortages in Norway, and I got my first (and last) taste of whale, the only meat available there at the time. Neither in Denmark or Norway did anyone talk about their lives during the war years.

There were, however, family tensions during the 1948 visit. Johanna, then seventy-seven, was no longer able to take care of herself, and Harald had shortly before arranged for her to live in an old-age home nearby in the Copen-hagen suburb of Charlottenlund instead of taking her into his own home. No love was lost between Johanna and her daughter-in-law Else or, for that matter, any of her daugh-ters-in-law. While living in Sweden in 1944, Johanna gave her opinion on that subject:

> Daughters-in-law are always jealous when sons are
> fond of their mothers. They do not understand that
> the love he has for his mother is something
> completely different from the love he has for his wife;
> this is about devotion, recognition and gratitude for
> what the mother has been to him for many years.
> Young people are eccentric, they are only thinking:
> 'Now it is my turn and nobody else may have a place
> in my husband's heart.'

Her letters were full of derogatory comments about Else.

When the war was over, Harald probably felt that he had done quite enough for Johanna, helping to get her out of Norway and then out of Denmark. She had lived with Else and himself in Copenhagen for a few months after she escaped from Norway, and it had not been a happy experience. Now Grete, visiting Denmark for the first time since the end of the war, unwisely threw herself into the dispute, telling Harald that he should have taken Johanna into his home. Another source of tension was that Harald had obtained a job at the Royal Danish Mint for Hjørdis, the ex-wife of his younger brother Alfred. Ignoring the fact that Harald had looked after Alfred's welfare, safety, and financial affairs for years, Grete did not conceal her opinion that Harald's hiring Hjørdis was an unfriendly act to his brother. Grete had not seen her relatives in Denmark for over a decade but this did not prevent her from actively taking sides in their family disputes.

In late May 1954, Jack and Grete left New York on the French liner *Liberté* for a two-month vacation in Europe. My sister Liz, then twenty and a junior in college, went with them. They left one sunny morning during the Memorial Day weekend. According to custom, there was a going-away party in the cabin of the ocean liner, which was docked at one of piers in the Hudson at around 50th Street. It was a pleasant and reasonably festive event, with no premonition of tragedy.

The European vacation had all the trappings of a Grand Tour. They traveled first class on what was probably the most luxurious ship crossing the Atlantic at the time. Caviar was spooned out generously. Dinner each evening was a formal occasion: passengers approached the dining room by descending a grand staircase. Some wore decora-

Grete and Jack with Johanna, Denmark, 1954.

tions and ribbons. Celebrities were on board: Liz remembers playing pingpong with the movie actor Richard Widmark (he was much nicer, she says, than he was in the sadistic roles he played: he was best known for the 1947 film *Kiss of Death,* in which he gleefully pushed an old woman in a wheelchair to her death down a staircase). They met Joe and his young wife, Mimi, in London, where Joe was working for our Uncle Sigi in the family fur business; and then all five proceeded to Paris, where Jack bought Grete clothes, scarves, and perfume. He was usually generous in material things.

After Paris, they spent a few days at the Palace Hotel in the Dutch seaside resort of Scheveningen. From that time on, there were signs that all was not well. One night there, Grete knocked at Liz's door (Liz had her own single room and Jack and Grete had a double room throughout the trip) and asked to spend the night. Mother and daughter lay next to each other for a while talking, but Grete did not explain why she had left her stateroom.

Jack was remote and even rude to Grete throughout the trip. He did not open doors for her but would walk ahead with Liz, leaving Grete to trot along behind. He also was especially cruel to Joe. Once, at a restaurant in Copenhagen with other family members (Max had come down from Oslo to meet them), after Joe's wife Mimi had ordered her dinner and Joe could not decide upon his, he said he would have whatever Mimi was having. Soon afterwards Mimi left the table briefly, and Jack berated Joe in the presence of the others for being subservient to his wife and having no mind of his own.

The next stop was Denmark, where they visited the home in Hellerup in suburban Copenhagen where Grete had lived as a young girl. They rang the doorbell and the occupants allowed them to enter. They visited Johanna in her nursing home; she was eighty-three and had become increasingly senile. Her failing mental and physical condition may well have deepened Grete's sadness. In a postcard to her sister Gerda on July 5, she wrote: "Will tell you all about mother when I return. It is difficult to tell in a letter." A photograph of Jack and Grete with Johanna on a Copenhagen park bench shows Johanna as a very old, shriveled woman.

But Grete did not appear depressed in Denmark. Her brother Harald wrote to Gerda a few weeks later: "Grethe was very nervous when she was here and talked incessantly, giving nobody else a chance to speak, but you know that she has always been like that . . . we perceived her as very self-confident, apparently believing that she could do no wrong."

After their visit to Denmark she sent Gerda cheerful postcards from Crans, in the Swiss Alps, where they spent two weeks golfing, saying that she was getting fat from all the good food in France, Holland, and Denmark.

When they returned to London, however, a strange thing happened. While Grete and Liz were repacking their clothes for the final time on their long vacation, Grete suddenly suggested that the two of them stay in London rather than return home to New York. Liz was astonished and replied that she was looking forward to returning to college. The only explanation Grete gave for wanting to remain in London (without Jack) was that she had come to hate New York, and was particularly bothered by its recent influx of noisy Puerto Ricans, who were changing the once-placid Manhattan.

This surprising proposal may have been Grete's last desperate attempt to save her own life. Perhaps she could no longer bear the thought of returning to her life with her husband in New York, with or without Puerto Ricans. But she must have realized that it was an impossible idea. Jack would never have permitted it, and she had no money of her own and no way of supporting herself in London. Most important, she lacked the psychological strength either to face him down or to divorce him. It is understandable that Liz was later haunted by the thought that she could have saved her mother by agreeing to stay with her in London. The truth is that it would never have happened, even if Liz had agreed.

On July 28, Jack, Grete, and Liz took the train to Southampton, where they embarked as first-class passengers on the Cunard luxury liner *R.M.S. Queen Elizabeth*. (Joe and Mimi stayed in England). The *Queen Elizabeth* was the largest passenger ship afloat. Named after King George VI's consort (later to be known for nearly half a century as the Queen Mother), the ship had been built just before the beginning of the war and had passed its first years as a troop transport. After the war, the *Queen Elizabeth* was refitted as a passenger liner and, along with its sister ship the *Queen Mary*, plied the busy and profitable five-day New York-to-Southampton run.

From the beginning, the *Queen Elizabeth* was an unlucky ship. During the two decades on the transatlantic run, it suffered two mysterious fires, ran aground outside Southampton, was immobilized in New York by labor disputes, and collided with a freighter outside New York harbor. After air travel made large passenger liners obsolete, it became a cruise ship for a few years, then was sold to a

Hong Kong company to be converted into a floating university. In 1972, another fire, caused by arson, destroyed the ship. Eventually, what was left of the *Queen Elizabeth* rolled over, spilling many tons of oil that polluted the Hong Kong beaches.[267]

In July 1954, however, the *Queen Elizabeth* was at the height of her fame and glory. On board on the crossing from Southampton to New York were 2,045 passengers, over 800 of them in first class. The first-class passengers included several celebrities, including the Metropolitan opera star Robert Merrill and his wife; Martin Niemoller, the German anti-Nazi clergyman; and Colonel Hubert F. Julian, an African-American aviator known as the "Black Eagle," who had previously been denied a passport for allegedly shipping arms from communist Poland to Guatemalan rebels.

Jack and Grete had a stateroom, which, like the rest of the *Queen Elizabeth*, was furnished in 1930s art deco style with light-colored wood. It had two portholes at roughly eye level, framed with colored curtains. Liz had a less luxurious single cabin on the inside of the ship.

After departing Southampton during the afternoon of July 28, the ship stopped at Cherbourg to pick up passengers, then set out on its five-day transatlantic journey. That evening, Jack, Grete, and Liz went to a movie, a Mexican musical with the well known actress Yma Sumac. Before the movie ended, Grete announced that she was tired and was going to bed. Although Liz didn't care for the movie, she stayed with Jack until it ended. Then they both went to their separate rooms.

At about 2:00 or 3:00 a.m. on July 29, Liz was awakened by Jack pounding on the door of her cabin. Was Grete with her? He must have known that it was impossible for her to be with Liz, because, when he awoke and found his wife missing, his cabin was still locked from the inside. Irrationally, he must have hoped that somehow she had left the cabin and was safe. Liz went with him back to his cabin. She noticed that, before going to bed, Grete had followed her usual habit of washing her stockings and hanging them up to dry in the bathroom. A chair was directly beneath the open porthole, which was not large and it was so high up that you needed to stand on a chair in order even to lean out. Jack had woken up shivering because of the open porthole. It was virtually impossible to fall from it accidentally, but it was large enough for an average-size woman to squeeze herself through.

Grete left no suicide note. She may have given a veiled warning to Alfred, her youngest brother. Shortly after her death, he wrote to Gerda: "Before the Posers left here, Grete asked me (twice) to keep her in my thoughts on July 28. When I asked her whether that was the day she would start on her return journey, she answered yes!" It is possible, however, that Alfred imagined this conversation.

Commodore C. I. Thompson, the ship's captain, was notified of Grete's disappearance. While the ship was searched, the captain ordered the ship turned back along its course for thirty miles in the highly unlikely hope of finding her in the sea. Jack told the captain that Grete had seemed depressed. There was no reason to believe any other explanation than that she had taken her own life. For many years Gerda refused to acknowledge that she committed suicide. Just possibly, she had opened the porthole and leaned out to get some air (she may have been in menopause and was having an unbearable hot flash) and somehow fallen out; but that explanation seems unlikely, considering the size and location of the porthole.

Liz stayed in her father's stateroom for the rest of the fatal night. She did not sleep but watched him silently lying in his bed, the thought crossing her mind that he too might decide to jump out. Neither then nor at any time later did Jack talk about Grete's death or what, if anything, had passed between them that night. He did not say whether she was asleep when he returned to the stateroom after the movie. Liz and he felt that they could not stay in the stateroom all the time, so sometimes they went up and paced the desk. Jack suggested that they count the number of steps they took.

NEW YORK DAILY MIRROR, *August 3, 1954. The caption read "Jack Poser . . . leaves liner with daughter Elizabeth, 21 (center) and an unidentified relative." The "unidentified relative" is Gerda.*

So they were silent or engaged in meaningless conversation for the next four days, a time of limbo for everyone, including family who waited in New York. When the *Queen Elizabeth* docked at Pier 90 on New York's West Side on August 2, newspaper reporters tried to interview Jack and Liz. The next day, the New York Daily News published a photograph of them disconsolately leaving the pier, with the caption: "Result of inquiry indicates [Margaret Poser] climbed through porthole and went overboard." The *Daily Mirror* wrote: "Poser and his daughter, sobbing continuously, refused to talk to newsmen. They were met at the pier by relatives and friends."[268]

Those relatives included me. At about 6:00 on the morning of July 29, I had been awakened by a call from a newspaper reporter who broke the news to me of Grete's disappearance from the *Queen Elizabeth*. I went back to bed and after a while decided to go out to buy some coffee. I felt nothing. The emotional numbness was something like that of the protagonist and narrator of Camus's *The Stranger* who said: "Maman died today. Or maybe yesterday. I don't know."

At the time of her death, Grete was fifty-two and Jack ten years older. He lived to be eighty-four, but I doubt he ever enjoyed a good night's sleep after that fatal crossing. It is likely that chronic depression, for which there was no effective treatment at the time, caused Grete to take her own life; but Jack's remoteness and (sometimes) hostility may also have contributed. If so, he suffered greatly for it.

Nora, Max's wife, obviously thinking about her own family's experiences during and after the war, wrote feelingly of Grete and her fate: "It is so sad that Grethe — who had every reason to have a wonderful life — still did not feel happy, perhaps even unhappier than all the rest of us who work so hard and who cannot enjoy the same material goods."

Unlike her mother, brothers, and sister, Grete did not have to escape from the Nazis. Yet the tragic end of her life was no less an escape — from a life that had become intolerable to her.

I still have letters Grete wrote me when I was in college. Today, I am surprised at how loving they were, because that is not how I experienced my mother at the time. For my part I had long learned to look elsewhere for love and affection, so was of no help to her. For many years after she died, I felt neither grief over her loss nor anger at Jack. Now, it is impossible not to feel great sorrow and pity for Grete.

⌈Aftermath⌋

Copenhagen, June 1948. Front row, Nora, Else, Johanna, Gerda (Alfred's wife). Back row, Lilian, Max, Harald, Norman.

The Salomon Family
After the War

EVEN BEFORE THE WAR ENDED, Johanna decided that she would live in Denmark when peace came rather than return to Norway. She gave Gerda four reasons for her decision: "Primarily the fact that I have become a Danish citizen,[269] secondly that I only lived through the hardest days of my life in Oslo, thirdly that I have no friends left there, and fourthly that I can no longer suffer the cold there." In early June 1945, less than a month after the end of the war, Johanna returned to Denmark. Because of the housing shortage, she spent a month in a camp for returning refugees, but she then took a room in a boarding house in Charlottenlund, the suburb of Copenhagen where her son Harald lived. In August 1945, she wrote to a friend in Norway:

> Now I am sitting here in lovely Charlottenlund,
> surrounded by gardens in bloom and the most
> beautiful flowers, everything is peace and quiet and I
> feel so incredibly happy. In the evening, when the sun
> is no longer so glaring, I go for a walk through the
> Charlottenlund Royal Park, looking at the castle

where our King [Christian X of Denmark] and King Haakon [Christian X's brother, Haakon VII of Norway] were born, and along the tree-lined road down to the Sound, where it is nice and cool and there are many sailors. Denmark certainly also has its charms!

Characteristically, Johanna waxed eloquent about the food she devoured in Denmark, despite some postwar shortages, and her extraordinarily detailed descriptions are indeed mouth-watering. In June 1946, she wrote to a friend in Norway:

The Pentacost holidays were completely ruined by a massive downpour, but we took some comfort in the delicious food we had [presumably at the boarding house]. The first day, we ate asparagus with melted butter (that we had saved up ahead of time), wienerschnitzel, and vanilla ice cream topped with two big strawberries per person. The second day, we were served chicken, new potatoes, and cucumber salad, followed by a cheese plate consisting of Roquefort, camembert, and Dutch cheese, lemon mousse. Not bad, or what do you think? After all, these are the only joys for us old folks.

Since food shortages in Norway were really severe in 1946, Johanna's willingness to share her delight in the food seems a little insensitive. However, she did send food packages to her friends, some of whom had shown her hospitality during the dark days when she lived in occupied Norway.

In late 1945, Johanna learned that one of her sisters, her sister's husband, and their two sons, whom she had thought had been killed in the Holocaust, had survived the war in Shanghai. They were equally delighted to find out that Johanna had survived the persecution of the Norwegian Jews. On the other hand, another sister and her daughter had vanished.

Despite generally weakening health and severe problems with her eyesight, she continued to take a detailed interest in the activities of here children and grandchildren. In November 1946, the family celebrated her 75th birthday. She wrote:

It was such a wonderful day! First, Max flew in [from Norway] on Saturday, which was a great surprise and joy. On Sunday morning, I received a lot of flowers, among them a lovely basket of pink roses from the Posers [in New York]. I was entirely thrilled by it. I have never before received such a flower gift in my whole life! Max brought a big bouquet of orange roses. Six ladies here at the guesthouse gave me a beautiful china bowl decorated with flowers, so now my room looks like one big flower store! There were many more flowers, too, including chrysanthemum, alpine violets, and magnificent orchid from the Palsbøls. We had dinner at the Skovridder Inn and coffee and a delicious supper at Harald's. So now everything is peace and harmony again. We have to forget the bad days. Harald gave me a tiny radio; they have become extremely expensive, and from Lilian, I got a very pretty handkerchief that she had sewn herself. At the dinner table, we had a toast to all our loved ones in the U.S.

Presumably, the "bad days" that Johanna wished to forget were not the days during the war but rather the family dissension between herself and Harald's wife, Else.

In 1947, Grete invited her mother to come and stay in New York for a year, but Johanna declined, saying: "I am old, hard of hearing and can only see with one eye. I am staying out here [in Charlottenlund] all the time; I only go into town when I need to see my lawyer regarding tax issues, but I really hate it, as I get confused by all the traffic – not to think of New York." Johanna entered an old-age home in 1948. She died in 1957, at the age of eighty-six.

When the war ended in 1945, Max and his family returned to their house in Nordstrand, where Max lived the rest of his life. Their house had been requisitioned by the German occupation authorities after Johanna was arrested in December 1942. Ironically, this was a benefit to them. Instead of the house being confiscated and sold at auction, it had been kept in good condition by its self-appointed German residents. Surprisingly, many of Max and Nora's possessions, including the linens and some of the furniture — and the silverware, which their housekeeper had buried under the gravel driveway — were still there. Some things, however, including their books, had been lost or stolen.

Although they had enough food and firewood for the winter, they were short of clothing, and there was nothing to buy in the Oslo stores. Ashamed of his shabby appearance, Max wrote to Gerda that he could use some fabric that could be made into a suit: "Perhaps Grete will treat me to one, so that I can finally have a suit made." Although Gerda was generous, sending him tobacco, chocolate, and other scarce items, he knew that the cost of these packages

Max and Nora after the war.

would come out of her slender income. Yet he apparently was reluctant to ask Grete directly for the fabric, even though she could easily afford to buy it. It is not clear whether Max received it.

It is surprising, after Max's success as an administrator of refugees in Sweden and the great satisfaction that he derived from this work, that he did not attempt to find a similar position when he returned to Norway. In the fall of 1945, he was pestered with doubts as to whether he should start his own business under the very difficult conditions that prevailed in Norway after the war, or apply for a position in public service. Soon after the war ended, he was offered what Nora described as a "good job," similar to the administrative position he had had in Sweden. He turned it down because it was not in Oslo but at Moss, a small city thirty-five miles from the capital on the east bank of the fjord.

Even while living in Sweden, Max had considered returning to his prewar business career. A year before the end of the war, he wrote to Gerda, asking her to ask Jack Poser what the prospects would be if he returned to the fur business in Norway. Again, it is curious why Max did not write directly to Jack or or Grete. Most likely, he felt somewhat estranged from them as a result of their lack of consideration for Gerda upon her arrival in New York. Perhaps, too, he believed that Gerda would be better able than Grete to talk to Jack about business affairs.

In any case, Jack was not encouraging about the fur business, and when Max did return to Oslo, he found that there were few business opportunities trading luxury goods such as furs. Moreover, after his escape to Sweden in 1940, a Norwegian company had moved into his office on Karl Johans Gate, and it took an eviction notice from the Municipal Authorities of Oslo to restore the property to Max Salomon.

Max began a business in leather goods, chiefly wallets and ladies' handbags; and for a few years he traveled around the country selling his merchandise. He hoped to do some export business with the United States, but that does not seem to have materialized. Max hated having to make sales pitches to customers, to such an extent that, according to his daughter, Frøydis, it made him seriously ill.[270] So eventually it was Nora who dealt with the customers, while Max largely confined himself to keeping the books. For a while the couple owned a handbag shop near the Oslo Town Hall. In 1960, they sold it and Max took a job with the Save the Children (the Norwegian name is "Redd Barna") organization, which he held until he retired at the age of seventy.

Max never received any restitution from the Norwegian government for the losses he sustained as a result of the war. However, in 1999, after Norway enacted a law providing compensation to Jews for the physical and economic losses they suffered during the war, Max's elder daughter Frøydis received 200,000 kroner. Her younger sister and her brother, who were not yet born in 1940 when Max and Nora fled Norway, received smaller amounts.

Max was an idealist, and the work he did for the public good, during the war in Sweden and afterwards in Norway, satisfied him deeply. He died in 1978, at the age of seventy-nine. Nora lived a very long life; she died in 1999, aged ninety-three.

Max could be considered unfortunate because he was more than forty years of age before his exile in Sweden enabled him to discover a line of work that was appropriate to his inclinations and talents. He nevertheless had the pleasure of seeing his three children in occupations that were to their liking. Frøydis, the oldest, is a university graduate and a librarian in Hamar, a city about 100 miles from Oslo. Her sister, Birgit, who is divorced, was educated at the Norwegian art and handicraft school and earns her living as an artist and art teacher. Robert, the youngest of Max and Nora's children, studied sociology. He is the director of the the Norwegian Institute for Labor Research. Max's six grandchildren are in a variety of professions, including law, journalism, and architecture; and there are eleven great-grandchildren, one of whom, at fourteen years of age, competes in Scandinavian schoolchildren's chess championships.

Norman with Max's children, Frøydis, Robert, and Birgit, in Norway, June 1948.

From left to right, Robert, Frøydis, Norman, and Birgit, in Norway, June 2004.

Although Gerda spent most of her long life in the United States, she always kept her close ties to Norway. She liked to talk about the history of the Salomon family and about her escape from Norway in 1940, but she never mentioned the persecution of the Norwegian Jews or Johanna's imprisonment in December 1942 and subsequent release.

For many years, Gerda lived in Bay Ridge, Brooklyn, which had a large Norwegian community. She supported herself and her daughter Dorrit by working as a x-ray technician and sometimes as a receptionist, first in a hospital and later for a medical group. Despite her modest income,

Gerda sent packages of cigarettes, food, tobacco, and clothing to her mother and brothers in Scandinavia during the difficult period of shortages that followed the war.

Gerda never remarried. She either ignored or found impractical her mother's advice on this and other subjects. In January 1946, Johanna wrote: "You might find an older bachelor or widower who could offer you and Dorrit a comfortable home, without any luxury, so that you could just live with him and Dorrit and wouldn't have to work so hard anymore." And a year later: "You wrote that [you and Dorrit] share a double bed, but I just heard that adults are *not supposed to sleep together* with their children as they are growing up, as the grownups are sucking energy from the young ones." One final example of Johanna's grandmotherly advice, this written in March 1947, when Dorrit was twelve: "As for Dorrit's teeth, I think they are really small. Does she eat a lot of soft white bread like they do in Sweden? I think you should feed her hard bread, such as crisp bread and dry biscuits, which would make her teeth work harder and hence develop more."

Despite her ability to make intelligent and independent decisions on the matters that deeply affected her life, Gerda was unfortunately an easy mark for predatory real estate salesmen. Twice she was induced to buy worthless plots of land, one in Pennsylvania and one in Connecticut; she paid monthly installments for years to banks that loaned her the purchase money. In the late 1970s, it became evident that her mind was failing, perhaps from Alzheimer's Disease. She spent the final twelve years of her life in an old-age home in New Paltz, New York, near where Dorrit lived.

In 1956, Dorrit married a Lutheran clergyman, Lloyd Berg, who also had a Norwegian background. From time to time, they visited Norway. Dorrit and Lloyd spent their summer vacations camping in national parks all over the United States, as well as in Canada, and Gerda usually went with them. Dorrit and Lloyd adopted three children, Kevin, Eric, and Sonia. At the time of their marriage, or perhaps even before then, Dorrit converted to Lutheranism. They were both active in the anti-Vietnam War movement. Sometime in the 1970s, however, they divorced and, as a result, Lloyd lost his parish. After that, he has worked for the Fellowship for Reconciliation, a pacifist organization, until he retired in 2005. After the divorce, Dorrit taught at the New York State University at New Paltz and lived with her partner, Nancy Stanich, until her death in November 2001.

Gerda too converted to Lutheranism. According to Lloyd, her conversion stemmed not from any religious conviction but from the fact that she found it more convenient to be Lutheran during the years that she was often with her daughter and son-in-law. Like all the other Salomons, Gerda had little interest in Judaism, or for that matter in any religion. She was simply a decent, affectionate, generous, and courageous person.

After the war, Harald returned to his position as medalist of the Danish Royal Mint, which he held until he retired in 1968. During the first few years after the war, he also kept his wartime affiliation with the Rörstrand Porcelain Factory in Sweden.

During the next few years, Harald was extremely active. He designed a new set of coins in 1947 to mark the accession of King Frederick IX to the Danish throne. During the 1950s and 1960s, he designed many commemorative coins and medals to mark royal birthdays and marriages.

*Harald's medal of Hans Christian Andersen
and the Ugly Duckling.*

He also designed medals to honor Hans Christian
Andersen, Niels Bohr, and other Danish artists and scien-
tists, and as well as world leaders such as Winston
Churchill and David Ben Gurion. He made beautiful expressive medals picturing himself, and his wife, daughter,
son-in-law, and grandson. According to his biographer:

> Harald Salomon's medal portraits are
> characterized by a great likeness to the sitter,
> meticulousness and an eye for detail, but he was
> capable of creating more than a 'realistic' rendition,
> which clients or viewers often expect from this genre.
> Salomon was always loyal to his sitter, and was able to
> examine closely while simultaneously remaining at a
> distance. As for the motifs and content of content of
> medals and coins, Salomon often chose genuinely
> Danish motifs, as some of his masters had trained
> him in their patriotic spirit.

Hardly any Danish artists have made a given genre their own to the same extent as Harald Salomon. For more than a quarter of a century, he created all the national coins and medals. Other domestic artists tried their hand at the art of medal-making, . . . but Salomon's output was so impressive that he virtually reigned supreme within his genre.[271]

Harald Salomon's work has been shown in museums throughout Denmark and elsewhere. In the 1960s, his work was exhibited at the Smithsonian Institution in Washington, D.C.; and in 1970 a major exhibition of his medals was held in Copenhagen to honor his seventieth birthday. After his retirement from the Mint in 1968, he continued to design medals and other works for a commercial company.

Harald (right) and Else at a banquet in Copenhagen.

Else died in 1975. She had been Harald's wife for fifty years. Harald continued to work in his studio in Charlottenlund well past his eightieth birthday. He died in 1990, at the age of ninety, a well loved and highly respected Danish artist. In 2000, to celebrate the centenary of his birth, a major exhibition of his work was shown in Copenhagen and later traveled to other parts of Denmark. A work that was specially mentioned in the catalog of the show was a charming bust of his daughter Lilian made in 1934, when she was one year old.

Lilian married Kulbir Birdi, a professor of chemistry who had immigrated to Denmark from India. They have a son named Leon, who is now married to Esma, a Dane of Turkish descent. In 2005, their first child (Harald's great-grandchild) was born.

After he was discharged as a mental patient from St. Hans Hospital in October 1945, Alfred struggled for many years to maintain a normal life. For a while he boarded with a clergyman in the country, where he worked as a farm laborer. During this time, his mother helped support him and bought him clothes and shoes, as his had been sold by his ex-wife during his hospital stay. In 1946, he moved back to Copenhagen, lived by himself, and took typing classes at night. For a time he worked as a debt collector for a large corporation. Alfred married again in 1947, and the following year he and his wife Gerda (not to be confused with his sister of the same name) had a son whose name was Jan. Alfred became the owner of a small trucking firm, while Gerda worked as a translator.

During the periods when Alfred's mental condition was stable, he was a caring and likable man. But he still suffered from manic-depression, which sometimes manifested itself in delusions and compulsive spending; and he was hospitalized for several periods during the 1950s and 1960s. Nevertheless, with the help of lithium and other mind-stabilizing drugs, Alfred continued operating his trucking business until he was seventy. Despite great stress caused by his mental illness, his second marriage endured. In 1976, he entered an old-age home in Copenhagen, where he remained until his death in 1997 at the age of ninety-three. His son Jan is said to be living in Germany, where he has worked as an airplane pilot.

My brother Joe served in World War II as a combat infantryman in New Guinea and the Philippines, where he was wounded in the shoulder. He was also in the occupation of Japan. After his discharge from the army, Joe entered the fur business with his father. He retired from the business a few years ago. He and his wife Mimi have three children: Margaret, who was born a few months after Grete's death and was named after her, is an art dealer; Nicholas is a lawyer with the Columbia Broadcasting System; and Daphne is a project manager for large construction projects. Joe and Mimi have three grandchildren, Nicholas and his wife April's children, Rachel, Justin, and Simon.

My sister Liz is a painter and printmaker who lives in Bridgehampton, New York. She and her husband Nat Gribin have three children, Eric, Elisa, and David. They have four grandchildren: Eric and his wife Maureen have two daughters, Sophie and Alanna; Elisa and her husband Michael Litchman have two sons, Joshua and Zachary. David is not currently married and has no children.

I am a law professor — that is when not writing a book about my mother's family. I have two children, Sam and

Susan, by my former wife, Miriam. Sam is a financial analyst and lives in Portland, Oregon. Strangely enough, Sam has followed his great-grandfather Simon Salomon's footsteps and is an expert in the shoe business. Possibly there is a shoe gene in the family's DNA that pops up every few generations. Susan has followed my footsteps and is a law professor in Lincoln, Nebraska. She is also an accomplished musician. I have two grandchildren, Susan and her husband Steve DiMagno's children, Eve and Sarah. My wife Judy also has two grandchildren.

THE SILENCE ABOUT THE HOLOCAUST that fol-
lowed the war is stunning. Although the systematic murder
of the European Jews by the Nazi government of Germany
was public knowledge as early as 1942, little was done to
document or commemorate the Holocaust until the 1960s,
when the capture and trial of Adolf Eichmann caught the
attention of the world. Study of the Holocaust did not
become an established part of the curriculum of schools in
Europe or the United States until the 1960s or 1970s, and
that often consisted solely of reading *The Diary of Anne
Frank*, in which a Jewish Dutch girl recorded her coming
of age while in hiding in Amsterdam.[272]

It was the same in Scandinavia. A curtain of silence
descended over the wartime experience of Norwegian and
Danish Jews; it did not begin to lift until the 1960s and
1970s. Norwegian and Danish collaborators with the Nazis
were tried for treason and other crimes committed during
the German occupation; but the trials, like the postwar
Nuremburg trials of the Nazi leaders, were not primarily
for atrocities against the Jews.

The role played by Norwegians in the persecution of the
Jews during the war became a taboo subject in Norway, and

few people outside the country were aware of the extent of Norwegian collaboration in persecution of the Jews. "After the war there were a great many stories about the heroic exploits of the resistance, but the true account of the Holocaust in Norway came out only much later."[273] For example, Thanks to Scandinavia, an organization formed in 1963 to express gratitude to the Scandinavians for saving Jews from the Holocaust, lumped together the wartime experience of the Jewish population of Norway with that of Denmark, although the experience of the Jews in the two countries was diametrically different. Thanks to Scandinavia speaks of "the singular acts of humanity and bravery of Denmark, Finland, Norway and Sweden in rescuing persons of the Jewish faith from the Holocaust,"[274] without distinguishing between the active participation of the Norwegian police and other government agencies in the murder of one-third of the Norwegian Jews in the winter of 1942-43 (although the Norwegian resistance enabled several hundred Jews to escape to Sweden in the winter of 1942-43) and the successful efforts of the Danish people to rescue virtually all the Danish Jews in October 1943.

It took more than half a century for Norway to begin to acknowledge the complicity of many Norwegians in the catastrophe visited upon Norwegian Jews during the German occupation. It was only in 1996 that the Norwegian Ministry of Justice appointed a committee to find out what happened to the property of Jews in Norway during World War II and what restitution was made after the war.[275] A year later, a divided committee issued a report, but a minority, consisting of Berit Reisel, a psychologist, and Bjarte Bruland, an historian, issued a dissenting report. The Norwegian Storting adopted the minority report, which took a much broader view of the harm done to the Jews during the occupation than did the majority report. The minority report pointed out that this harm consisted not only of the confiscation of property and "economic liquidation" but also restriction of rights, segregation and isolation, deportation, and physical liquidation. In 1999, the Storting authorized payments totaling 450 million kroner as restitution of Jewish economic losses. Today, the Holocaust is taught in Norwegian schools, and as part of this education some schoolteachers take groups of high school students on field trips to the German concentration camps.

However inexcusable it may be, the silence that prevailed in Norway for so long is easy to understand. Although members of the Norwegian resistance movement performed acts of heroism in hiding Jews and helping them escape to Sweden, Norway had a strong motivation to forget or cover up the existence of its own concentration camps in which Jews were mistreated, tortured, and killed; and the cooperation — and in some cases enthusiasm — of the Norwegian police and civil service in depriving one-third of the Norwegian Jews of their rights and property, arresting them, and turning them over to the Germans for deportation and death. Furthermore, there is no reason to suppose that the vicious anti-Semitism endemic in Norway for centuries disappeared after the war, although it was no longer acceptable to express these feelings publicly.

If the postwar silence in Norway is easy to explain, the silence in Denmark is much more puzzling. The Danish people collectively performed a unique act of heroism in rescuing the great majority of Danish Jews from deportation and death in October 1943. The Holocaust Museum in Washington, D.C., honors not only Danish individuals but "The Danish People" on its wall of righteous persons who saved Jews from the Holocaust. This was an action for which Denmark can justly be proud.

Yet the Danes did not proclaim their own heroism, and their rescue of the Danish Jews was not generally known about during the immediate postwar years. One reason the Danes were silent was shame over their government's cooperation with Germany during the first three and a half years of the occupation.[276] According to a recent article, the Danish government expelled twenty-one stateless Jewish refugees to Germany during the period 1940-43.[277] Another reason was that, in accordance with their democratic principles, they did not wish to stress the difference between Jews and non-Jews."[279] Not only Jews but other anti-Nazi Danes were rescued from deportation to German concentration camps.

A large book of photographs published in Malmö, Sweden, in 1946 to commemorate the occupation of Denmark and the Danish resistance movement fails even to mention the rescue of the Jews, which has since become famous throughout the world. Two of the book's photographs show small boats crossing the Øresund to Sweden in October 1943; the caption of one of the pictures states that "a steady stream of refugees" was crossing to Sweden, without any reference to the fact that almost all the refugees were Jews threatened with deportation to Germany.[279]

Harold Flender, the author of a book that first brought the Danish Rescue into American public consciousness in 1963, states that he first learned about it in 1961 from testimony given at the trial in Jerusalem of Adolf Eichmann, the SS commander who directed the implementation of the Final Solution. The testimony was that of David Melchior, the son of Marcus Melchior, the acting chief rabbi of Copenhagen in 1943.[280] Before the Eichmann trial, to my knowledge only one account of the rescue had been published, a book by Aage Bertelsen, a Danish clergyman and teacher who had helped organize it. Although Bertelsen's book was published in English in 1954, it attracted little public attention. The Danish Rescue did not become a legend of the Holocaust until the 1970s and later, when many books, including some aimed at young readers, and museum exhibitions told the world about the event.

Part of the reason the Danes did not want to celebrate the rescue may have been the brief flare-up of anti-Semitism that occurred in that country immediately after the war.[281] There was resentment that the rescue of the Jews was organized by non-Jews, the Jews leaving others to do the rescue work.[282] There also was resentment that some Danish Jews of military age chose not to join the 5,000-man Danish Brigade, which was organized in Sweden in order to participate in the liberation of Denmark.[283] Furthermore, the Danes place a high premium on social conformity, and there was resentment after the war that, while most Danish Jews became (or remained) highly assimilated into Danish society, some whom they rescued continued to observe their own customs and rituals, rather than blending in with Danish culture.[284] Many Danish Jews left the country and emigrated to Israel or the United States in the years following the war.

The members of the Salomon family who had fled Norway and Denmark during the war also remained silent about their experiences, even with their close relatives. The next generation (including myself), who were children during the war, were told very little about what happened to the family. One illustration of how ignorant the postwar generation was kept about the family's wartime experience may be mentioned here. In doing research for this book, I was at first puzzled by the fact that my grandmother, Johanna, was living in *Oslo* when the Germans invaded in April 1940 but escaped to Sweden from *Copenhagen* in October 1943. How, when, and why did she travel from occupied Norway to occupied Denmark? Neither Max's daughter Frøydis in Norway nor Harald's daughter Lilian in Denmark could tell me. Although Johanna's sons Max and Harald knew that in 1942-43 she had been imprisoned for three months in Norway and narrowly escaped being deported to Auschwitz, they seem never to have told their children about it. Nor do I recall my mother or my aunt Gerda telling me of Johanna's imprisonment and double escape (from Norway and later from Denmark), although they too knew about it, as Max's letters to Gerda in early 1943 attest. Nor was it mentioned by anyone (including Johanna herself) when I visited Denmark and Norway in 1948, only three years after the end of the war.

I learned of Johanna's imprisonment only when I came into possession of a letter Max wrote to Gerda from Sweden in January 1943 describing in some detail what had happened; and I first learned about the successful efforts of the Danish consul in Oslo to obtain her release from prison from Bjarte Bruland, a Norwegian historian of the Holocaust. It was only after gaining access to the archives of the Danish Ministry of Foreign Affairs that it was possible to piece together these events and learn that upon her release from prison in Norway Johanna returned to Copenhagen, only to escape from Denmark a few months later. This is just one example of the silence that has surrounded the partly heroic and partly shameful story of the war against the Jews of Scandinavia.

It is likely that the Salomon family's silence about the war years, which enormously disrupted their lives, was due in large part to a desire to put these hard times behind them and to get on with their lives. Another reason may have been their reluctance to emphasize their Jewish heritage. Max was born in Norway, lived most of his life there, and always felt himself to be a Norwegian. When the war was over, he consciously decided to shed any identity as a Jew. Harald, who was able to resume his successful career after the war, was more self-confident about his Jewish background, and furthermore fortunate to live in the more tolerant atmosphere of Denmark. Both, however, were unwilling to dwell on the war and the occupation, which had singled them out for punishment only because they were Jewish. To their descendants, their Jewish heritage seems no longer of any importance or even interest. It is of course up to each person whether he or she wishes to be part of a religious community. Let us hope that world events do not again single out persons of Jewish descent for persecution, whether or not they practice a religion. This is not an idle or irrelevant sentiment, for anti-Semitism is again on the rise in Europe, and Scandinavia is not immune from it.

———◆———

SALOMON was not an uncommon Jewish family name in northern Germany and Scandinavia during the nineteenth century. The earliest known member of the Salomons who are the subject of this book was Wolf Salomon (1800-82) and his wife Fanny (née Marcus) (1804-82), who are buried in the Jewish cemetery in Kiel, the largest city in the German state of Schleswig-Holstein. Kiel was part of the Duchy of Holstein, which was under Danish rule until 1864.

It is not certain that Wolf and Fanny Salomon were the parents of Marcus Wolf Salomon, who was born in Altona, another city in Holstein, on April 1, 1828. That it is likely is supported by Fanny Salomon's maiden name, by Marcus Salomon's middle name, and by the date of his birth, when Wolf Salomon was 28 and his wife was 24.

Marcus's wife was Emma Levin (or Lewin), who was born in Leck, a small town in Schleswig (now part of Germany), on September 8, 1826, although the inscription on her tombstone in Oslo indicates that she was born in 1821. It is unlikely, but possible, that she was born in 1821 because she would have been seven years older than her husband and 45 when her youngest child was born.

It can be deduced that Marcus and Emma lived in Kiel in the early 1850s and that they moved to Copenhagen between 1853 and 1856. Birth records show that their first child was born in Kiel in 1853 and that their second child was born in Copenhagen in 1856.

Marcus and Emma moved to Stockholm in 1879, and Marcus became a Swedish citizen in 1884. He died in Hamburg in 1891, apparently having become a German citizen. Altona, Marcus's birthplace, became part of Germany in 1864, and it is likely that persons who were born in the annexed territories were able to assume German citizenship. Emma likewise lived in Hamburg in the early 1890s, and she was described as a German citizen when she was registered in Oslo in 1894 as one of the owners of Salomon & Son. Emma died in Oslo in 1906.

In addition to Siegmund and Simon, whose lives are described in the body of the book, Marcus and Emma had three other children: Salomon Marcus, Levy (or Leopold), and Betty Cecilia.

Salomon Marcus was born in Kiel on June 2, 1853. Perhaps because he had the same first and last names, he was called by his nickname, Sally. This has caused some researchers to believe mistaken-ly that Sally was a girl. As a child, he lived in Copenhagen with his parents. He worked in Kiel as an apprentice to a merchant and later moved to Hamburg. He married Marta Clara Kelm, who was born in Berlin in 1853. They had one child, Hermione Else Mathilde, who was born in Hamburg in 1879. In 1879 or 1880, Sally and Marta moved to Gothenberg, Sweden.

In Gothenburg, Salomon Marcus became the manager of a men's clothing store owned by Levy Samson (also known as Louis Samson), a Norwegian businessman, with the understanding that he would eventually take over the store. He became a Swedish citizen in 1883.

Levy Samson, Salomon Marcus's employer in Gothenburg, was one of the earliest Jewish settlers in Norway. Born in Schleswig-Holstein in 1839, he must have known Marcus Salomon in the 1850s when they both were members of Kiel's small Jewish population. Samson immigrated to Norway in 1860, only nine years after Jews were first permitted to enter the country. In Oslo, he first worked for a Norwegian tailor, but two years later he obtained a license to engage in business for himself under the name of L. Samson & Company. By the early 1880s, he also owned a clothing factory as well as a clothing and shoe store in Oslo. Sally worked at a branch of this store that Samson opened in Gothenburg.

Levy Samson became a rather prominent resident of Oslo. In 1862, he married a non-Jew from Schleswig, Marie Wichmann, and they had ten children. He took an important role in many business projects in Norway, including the building of an electric trolley line, and he contributed to many charitable causes. Samson also had an interesting and unusual sideline: he was probably the only Jewish diplomat in Norway in the nineteenth century; beginning in 1880, he served as the consul in Oslo for the State of Hawaii, which was an independent country until the United States annexed it in 1897.[285] His son, W.B. Samson, established a famous Oslo bakery, which still exists over a century later; it baked the wedding cake for Crown Prince Haakon and Princess Mette-Marit in 2001.

In 1880, Salomon Marcus became the owner of Levy Samson's Gothenburg clothing store; and his younger brother, Siegmund, worked with him in the store, either as a partner or employee. In view of the family's background in the shoe business, it seems likely that the Gothenburg store sold shoes, and perhaps also made and repaired them. Salomon Marcus died at the age of forty, still a Swedish citizen, in Malmö, Sweden, in 1893. Two years later, Martha Clara was living in Bad Segeberg, a tourist town in southern Holstein, and that is the last we hear about her.[286]

Levy (or Leopold) Marcus Salomon, Marcus and Emma's second child, was born in Copenhagen on September 8, 1856. He does not appear to joined the family business; rather, like several other members of the family, he had an artistic bent. At least, we know that he played the violin. Like several other family members, he suffered from mental illness, and at some point his father committed him to an insane asylum in Austria that was run by a Fremason Lodge.[287] That is the last we hear of him.

Betty Cecilia Salomon, Marcus and Emma's only daughter, was born in Copenhagen on October 2, 1866. She lived with her parents in Copenhagen and later in Stockholm. Her whereabouts during the late 1880s and early 1890s are unknown, but it is possible that she lived in Hamburg with her parents after they moved there. By 1894, was living in Oslo with her mother and her older brother, Siegmund. Like her brother, Leopold, Betty suffered from mental disease. In 1894, she was committed to the Gaustad insane asylum, located on the outskirts of Oslo. The asylum had been founded in 1855 as a response to increasing concern about the care of the mentally diseased. It was the first modern mental institution in Norway, modeled on the asylum in the French city of Auxerre. The idea was to provide fresh air, natural surroundings, and activities for the patients. In conformity to the class distinctions of the time, Gaustad had separate facilities for the so-called educated classes and for the poor. It is likely that Betty was assigned to the former.

Betty died at Gaustad on November 5, 1894, at the age of twenty-eight. She was unmarried and had few personal belongings. The records of the asylum have been destroyed, so neither the specific reason for her commitment to Gaustad nor the cause of her death is known. However, the much later Danish hospital records of Betty's nephew, Alfred Salomon, provide information about other members of the family. These records state that Alfred's paternal aunt was suicidal. Betty was Alfred's only paternal aunt, so this entry suggests that she committed suicide at Gaustad.[288]

Betty's death led to a bitter dispute within the Jewish community in Oslo. Betty was buried in the Jewish cemetery in the Sofienberg section of Oslo, which was owned by the Mosaic Congregation, one of the two Jewish congregations into which Oslo's small Jewish population was divided. A year after her death, Siegmund had become the president of the Israelite Congregation, the other Jewish congregation. He and Simon tried to reserve grave sites for themselves beside their sister's grave. Unfortunately, a woman from Trondheim named Lisa Gittelson was already buried in this space. The president of the Mosaic Congregation gave them permission to move Lisa Gittelson's coffin to another site, but a member of the congregation asked a rabbi in Lübeck, Germany, whether this was allowed under rabbinical law. The rabbi replied that it was forbidden to remove a body from a grave unless ordered to do so by the civil authorities.

Nevertheless, the Salomons removed the coffin without authorization, to the consternation of the other members of the congregation. A relative of the late Lisa Gittelson reported their action to the police, and the board of the congregation gave the brothers the choice of paying a 1,000 kroner fine, a substantial sum at the time, or finding another graveyard in return for the reserved grave sites.[289] They must have paid the fine, for Betty and her mother Emma are both buried under a handsome obelisk-like monument in the Sofienberg cemetery.

ENDNOTES

1 Norman, p. 6.
2 Kuhl, p. 26.
3 Dinse, §3.2.7.
4 After Prussia annexed Schleswig-Holstein in 1864, Altona lost its separate identity and became a suburb of Hamburg.
5 *Encyclopedia Britannica,* vol. 1, p. 764-65 (11th ed. 1911).
6 Emma's tombstone in Oslo states that her maiden name was Lewin and that she was born in 1821. This birthdate seems unlikely (although possible) because it would make her seven years older than Marcus and 45 years of age when her youngest child, Betty, was born in 1866. Furthermore, the birth records of her two younger sons indicate that she was 33 years of age in July 1858 and 35 in December 1860, indicating that Emma was born in 1824 or 1825.
7 Steefel, p.3, n.1.
8 The Sudeten Germans were ethnic Germans who became citizens of Czochoslovakia under the Versailles Treaty ending World War I. In 1938, the British Prime Minister Neville Chamberlain tried to appease Adolf Hitler by bowing to his demand to annex the Sudentenland in the infamous Munich Pact.
9 Gallenga, p.50.
10 Steefel, p. 7.
11 Westegaard, p. 26.
12 Steefel, pp.7-8. The battle, which was fought on July 6, 1849, pitted 41,000 Danes against 65,000 German Schleswig-Holsteiners. Westegaard, p. 52.
13 Gallenga, p.3.
14 The commander of the Danish army, General C. J. de Meza, was Jewish. Jewish Life in Scandinavia (SAS pamphlet).
15 There were two Danish-German wars, the first in 1848 and the second in 1864. In the second war, the Schleswig-Holsteiners, supported by the Prussian and Austrian armies, defeated Denmark. Through military might and diplomatic skill, Bismarck's Prussia succeeded in annexing all of Schleswig-Holstein in 1864. It was not until 1920, in the wake of World War I, that Denmark succeeded in regaining the northern, primarily Danish-speaking, portion of Schleswig.
16 Dinse, §5.3.1.
17 Bamberger, p. 50-51.
18 Yahil, pp. 7-8.
19 Quoted in Garff, p. 535.
20 Garff, pp. 536-39.
21 The square gets one star as a sightseeing attraction in the *Michelin Green Guide.*
22 Unfortunately, there seems to be no English translation of Wessel's play.
23 A census of the city of Stockholm in 1881 shows Marcus and Emma Salomon, their son Simon, aged 21, and their daughter Betty Cecilia, aged 15, all living at the same address.
24 The records in Hamburg identify Marcus as a "kaufman,"

a word that can be translated as either a merchant, trader, or storekeeper. Information supplied by Professor Ole Harck from Hamburg archives.

25 The date of Simon Salomon's arrival in Oslo is stated in the municipal census of Dec. 31, 1905. Email dated Aug. 13, 2002, from Leif Thingsrud to the author.

26 Norman, p. 17. There was still a Salomon shoe store in Bodø in northern Norway in 2005.

27 Storing, pp. 23-25.

28 Kisch.

29 Spain did not permit Jews to settle there until 1869, but even then they could become citizens of the country only under specific conditions. Gerber, pp. 258-60.

30 It is possible to overstate the difference in the two countries' attitudes toward the Jews. The rights that Denmark gave in 1814 were only for Danish Jews; foreign Jews still had to obtain permission if they wished to remain in the country. Until 1850, the Danish authorities maintained a special registry for foreign Jews but not for other foreigners. H. Jørgensen (ed.) Indenfor murene. Jødisk liv i Danmark 1684-1984. København 1984.

31 For a period during the seventeenth century, Jews were permitted to travel freely in Norway, but this permission was rescinded by the Danish King Christian V in 1687. Records of the Mosaic Religious Community in Norway.

32 Storting, p. 25.

33 Conversation between Bjarte Bruland and the author, July 20, 2004.

34 Hellig, pp. 214-16.

35 Bjørnstad, pp. 34-53.

36 Abrahamsen, p. 26. O. Mendelsohn, *Jødenes historie I Norge* gjennon 300 år Volume 1. Oslo 1987 (1969).

37 Hugo Valentin, *Antisemitism Historically and Critically Examined* (1936) (quoted in Abrahamsen, p. 24).

38 Abrahamsen, p. 26.

39 Abrahamsen, p. 27.

40 Mendelsohn, *Jødenes Historie I Norge*, p. 275.

41 Levy Samson, an enterprising businessman who moved to Oslo from Kiel in 1860, may have influenced Siegmund Salomon's decision to emigrate. Samson established a clothing store in Oslo, which had a branch in Gothenburg, Sweden. Siegmund and his elder brother Sally both worked at the Gothenburg store during the 1880s, and Sally may have owned the store after Levy Samson retired.

42 Marta Gjernes, "Dei fyrste jødiske innvandrarfane i Kristiania" in *Historisk Tidskrift*, Vol. 43, No. 3, pp. 385-416.

43 Benkow, pp. 11-12.

44 A shoe factory established in Bergen in 1881 was the first to use industrial production methods. E.W. Erichsen (ed.), *Norsk kotøyindustri i 50 år.* Oslo 1951.

45 The origins of the Salomon shoe factory are set forth in

E.W. Erichsen (ed.), *Norske skotøyhistorie i 50 år* (Norwegian Shoe Industry Through 50 Years), Oslo 1951..

46 Oslo Regional State Archives. I have this information from Marta Gjernes.

47 Hunger, p. 90.

48 Derry, p. 188.

49 Popperwell, p. 36.

50 Derry, pp. 191-96.

51 The factory was still in operation in 1951. Email dated Sept. 1, 2002, from Ragnar Areklett to the author.

52 Norman, p. 18.

53 When the business was incorporated in 1898, its initial capital was 400,000 kroner, which were divided into 800 shates having a nominal value of 500 kroner.

54 Norman, p. 19.

55 The information about the Salomons' labor disputes was obtained by Ragnar Areklett from the Archives of the Norwegian Labor Movement. Email dated Nov. 13, 2002 from Ragnar Areklett to the author.

56 K. Kjeldstadli, Part III. 1901-1940, in K. Kjeldstadli (ed.) *Norsk innvandringshistorie,* Volume 2, I Nasjonalstatens tid, Oslo 2003.

57 Norman, p. 19.

58 Norman, p. 63.

59 *Flagpole Magazine,* Feb. 11, 1998, p. 12.

60 Max's middle name led to some confusion in my Aunt Gerda's mind. When I questioned her in 1970 about the history of the family, she told me that her grandfather's name was Marcus de Sola Salomon, and that she thought the name of Marcus's mother's family was de Sola and that they were Sephardic Jews from Spain. In fact, Marcus's middle name was Wolff, and his mother's maiden name probably was Fanny Wolff. Gerda apparently confused her grandfather Marcus with her older brother Max (officially Marcus), whose middle name was Zola.

61 *Tidens Tegn* was a moderate liberal newspaper that was founded in 1910 by one of Norway's most outstanding journalists and editorial talents, Olaus Anton Thomessen (1851-1942). Despite the newspaper's liberalism, it was in *Tidens Tegn* that Vidkun Quisling, announced the formation of his Nazi-affiliated Nasjonal Samlung (National Unification) party in May 1933. Ironically, the paper closed down in 1942 because it did not sufficiently support the Norwegian Nazis. Quisling was hanged as a traitor in 1946.

62 Bjørnstad, p. 128.

63 Simpson, p. 217.

64 The house had a rather notorious subsequent history. It was occupied by the German occupation authorities during the war; after that it became a famous brothel, which was used as the background for a popular novel exposing the prostitution business, entitled *You'll Never Have My Thoughts;* and a later owner of the house was convicted of diamond

smuggling. This was told to me by one of the present occupants and by my cousin Robert Salomon.

65 Norman, pp. 16-17.

66 Harvey & Reppien, p. 36.

67 Harvey & Reppien, p. 313.

68 Max and Nora's grandchildren — and their children — still live in the house. In the 1970s, Max's son Robert built a smaller house next door, where he and his wife Sissel live today.

69 Mirjam Gelfer-Jørgensen, "Jewish Art in the 20th Century," in Mirjam Gelfer-Jørgensen, ed., *Danish Jewish Art*, p. 550 (Rhodos, Copenhagen 1999).

70 Catalog for the exhibition of Harald Salomon's medals held in 1970 in the Medal Room of the Royal Coin and Medal Collection in Copenhagen to celebrate his 70th birthday.

71 Yahil, op. cit., pp. 327-30; Wulschlager, pp. 389-426.

72 Else Rasmussen, Harald Salomon: en dansk medaljor og billedhugger (Harald Salomon: A Danish Medalist and Sculptor) (2002), p. 12.

73 Harvey & Reppien, pp. 37.

74 Rasmussen, p. 7.

75 Norman, pp. 37, 43.

76 Norman, p. 49.

77 Norman, pp. 61-62.

78 Richard Petrow, "The Bitter Years: The Invasion and Occupation of Denmark and Norway April 1940-May 1945," p. 102 (London 1974).

79 Bjørnstad, p. 220.

80 Laquer, p. 446.

81 Laquer, p. 446. Information provided by Marta Gjernes.

82 Abrahamsen, p. 43.

83 Files of the Danish Consulate in Oslo (Dec. 2, 1938).

84 Article by Ledon Jarner in *Verdens gang* (Nov. 29, 1945) (republished in The Reisel/Bruland Report on the Confiscation of Jewish Property in Norway during World War II, p. 99 (June 1997).

85 Danish State Archives, File No. 130.N.9.

86 Reisel/Bruland Report, p. 1; Dawidowicz, pp. 48—69.

87 Laquer, p. 451.

88 Bjarte Bruland, "Victims of the Shoah in Norway."

89 Laquer, p. 449.

90 Bruland, p. III.

91 Danish State Archives, File No. 104.N.33.e.

92 Abrahamsen, p. 105.

93 Bjarte Bruland, *Victims of the Shoah in Norway.*

94 Mendelsohn, p. 11.

95 The Danish Consulate in Oslo immediately sent copies of the order to Danish Ministry of Foreign Affairs. Danish State Archives, File No. 130.N.9.

96 Mendelsohn, pp. 11-12.

97 Mendelsohn, pp. 15-16.

98 Bruland, "Victims of the Shoah" in *Norway,* p. IV.

99 Public Notice dated Febraury 1

100 Circular Letter, dated November 17, 1942, from the Norwegian Ministry of the Interior (Dept. of Ordinary Affairs) to all Regional Commissioners, entitled ""Jews' Duty of Report."

101 Marthinsen was assassinated by the Norwegian resistance in

February 1945.

102 Abrahamsen, p. 120.

103 Laquer, p. 450, Abrahamsen, p. 76.

104 Laquer, p. 451.

105 In 1940, the Gestapo instructed: "As far as possible, the Norwegian police should be allowed to carry out the measures we want implemented." Laquer, p. 448.

106 Laquer, p. 450.

107 Email dated July 6, 2002, to the author from Ragnar Areklett, who has written about the deportation of the Norwegian Jews; Abrahamsen, p. 100.

108 Mendelsohn, pp. 12-13.

109 Email dated Mar. 13, 2003, to the author from Ragnar Areklett, recounting a statement by Sara Mahler Uthaug, who was sent to Bredtvedt some months after Johanna's release from the prison.

110 Abrahamsen, p. 111.

111 Mendelsohn, p. 16.

112 Today, Bredtvedt is the largest women's prison in Norway, with about 50 inmates. Thanks to the help of Ragnar Areklett, my wife and I were given a guided tour of the prison in June 2004. It appears to be devoted to the goal of rehabilitation rather than punishment, and contains a variety of facilities, such as sports and exercise facilities, a multi-language library, computers, and a chapel.

113 Emails dated Mar. 13, 2002 and July 8, 2002, from Ragnar Areklett to the author; email dated Oct. 5, 2002, from Victor Lind to the author.

114 Museum of the Resistance, Oslo.

115 Petrow, p. 116.

116 Only the Catholic bishop of Norway refused to sign the letter. He said that he would only protest the arrest of Jews who had converted to Catholicism. It is not clear whether he made even this protest. Telephone conversation with Bjarte Bruland (July 20, 2004).

117 Petrow, p. 116.

118 Quisling's speech was reported by the Danish consul-general in Oslo to the Danish Ministry of Foreign Affairs.

119 Abrahamsen, p. 8.

120 Petrow, p. 330.

121 By contrast, some Norwegian policeman did disobey orders to arrest schoolteachers who had refused to join the Quisling government's Teachers' Front in early 1942 and were sent to labor camps in northern Norway. Petrow, pp. 111-14; telephone conversation with Bjarte Bruland (July 20, 2004).

122 Mr. Areklett became interested in the story of the deportation of the Norwegian Jews when he visited the Theresienstadt concentration camp near Prague in 1995. He writes: "Suddenly a question struck me: What had happened to the Jewish family [named Fischer] who lived in our neighborhood, and the youngest boy [with whom] I had played together." He later learned that almost the entire family had been killed in Auschwitz. Email dated July 8,

2002, from Ragnar Areklett to the author.

123 Petrow, p. 116; Abrahamsen, pp. 111-12.

124 Telephone conversation with Bjarte Bruland (July 20, 2004).

125 Valentin, p. 233; Abrahamsen, p. 12..

126 ronically, the leader of Nansen Aid in the Ukraine was Vidkun Quisling, then a Norwegian army captain. Derry, p. 340.

127 Petrow, p. 364.

128 Laquer, p. 446.

129 According to one historian of the Holocaust in Norway, an estimated 50,000 Norwegians, including 925 Jews, escaped to Sweden during the German occupation. Abrahamsen, p. 2.

130 Bruland, *Victims of the Shoah in Norway,* p. I.

131 Reisel/Bruland Report, p. ix.

132 Abrahamsen, p. 1; Bruland, Victims of the Shoah in Norway, p. I; Reisel/Bruland Report, p. ix; Westlie (1995); Dawidowicz, pp. 369-71.

133 Mendelsohn, p. 28.

134 Mendelsohn, p. 28.

135 Abel Abrahamsen, speech at Scandinavia House in New York, Jan. 16, 2003.

136 Mendelsohn, p. 28; Valentin, p.231.

137 Abrahamsen, pp. 109-10.

138 Derry, p. 391.

139 A few months after Johanna's arrest, the Germans, who had been eying Vikersund Bad as an attractive place for a district headquarters, threw the remaining doctors and patients out and took it over.

140 On October 26, 1942, a law was passed by the Norwegian Nazi government authorizing the confiscation of Jewish property. 140 Laqueur, p. 450.

141 The last major transport of Norwegian Jews occurred on February 24, 1943, with the prison ship *Gotenland,* which had 158 Jews aboard. Mendelsohn, p. 22.

142 Danish State Archives, File No. 3.G.75.

143 A list of the Danish MFA dated February 26, 1943, contains the names of eleven Danish Jews and one half-Jew in Norway. 144 Danish State Archives, File No. 104.N.33.e.

144 The actions taken by the Norwegian government against the Jews and the concerns expressed by the Danish Jews in Norway are described in detail in a memorandum dated January 25, 1943, from Schrøder to the MFA, entitled "Measures taken against Jews in Norway" and marked "Strictly Confidential!" The memorandum lists eight "full Jews of Danish nationality currently residing in Norway who might be considered for the granting of entry visas to Denmark," including Johanna Salomon and her nephew Hans Salomon. Hans's wife Gunvor is also listed as a non-Jew. Danish State Archives, File No. 130.N.9.

145 Danish State Archives, File No. 84.G.11.

146 Danish State Archives, File No. 84.G.11.

147 Danish State Archives, File No.

84.g.11.

148 Danish State Archives, File No. 84.G.11.

149 Arendt, p. 154.

150 Danish State Archives, File No. 35,K.569.

151 Danish State Archives, File No. 16.J.91.

152 Danish State Archives, File No. 16.J.91.

153 Danish State Archives, File No. 35.K.569.

154 Danish State Archives, File No. 130.N.9.

155 Danish State Archives, File No. 35.K.572.

156 Danish State Archives, Files No. 84.G.11; 130.N.9.

157 Danish State Archives, File No. 84 G. 11.

158 Danish State Archives, File No. 84 G. 11.

159 Danish State Archives, File No. 140.N.33.b/182.

160 Letter dated June 26, 1945. Danish State Archives, File. No. 3 G.75.

161 *New York Times,* Jan. 7, 1946, p. 7; *New York Times,* Mar. 9, 1947, p. 38.

162 Bruland, Victims of the Shoah in Norway, p. III.

163 Mendelsohn, p. 21.

164 Mendelsohn, p. 22.

165 Stettin is now part of Poland and is renamed Szczecin.

166 Abrahamsen, p. 122.

167 Petrow, p. 116.

168 Abrahamsen, p. 124.

169 Mendelsohn, p. 24.

170 Reisel/Bruland Report, p. ix.

171 Reisel/Bruland Report, p. ix.

172 Speech by Bjarte Bruland, Scandinavia House, New York, Jan. 16, 2003.

173 Westlie.

174 In 1940, one U.S. dollar was the equivalent to 4.4 Norwegian kroner, and the U.S. Consumer Price Index increased about 13 times between 1940 and 2003. www.eh.net/hmit/exchangerates e. This, however, seems to give an unduly conservative picture of American inflation. For example, the cost of the daily *New York Times* rose from 33 times (3¢ to $1) and a New York subway or bus ride rose 40 times (5¢ to $2) during this period.

175 Reisel/Bruland Report, pp. 12-13, 28-29.

176 The information about Røed (or Rød) was provided to me by Victor Lind, a Norwegian who gathered the information from official archives. Email dated Oct. 5, 2002 from Victor Lind to the author.

177 Siegmund and Melitta Salomon lived separately for most of the interwar years, although they remained married. Norman, p. 23.

178 Danish State Archives, File No. U.4239.

179 Report by the Norwegian State Police on "Release of the Jew Hans Salomon from Berg Internment Camp" (Feb. 22, 1943), Reference:)V 5000/42.

180 Danish State Archives, File No. 130.N.9.

181 Danish State Archives, File No. 84.g.11.i.

182 Danish State Archives, File No. 140.N.33.b/18.

183 Petrow, pp. 74-77.

184 Abrahamsen, pp.71-72; Petrow,

p. 96.

185 Abrahamsen, pp. 4, 15-23; Laqueur, p. 446, 450-51.

186 Nordlund, p. 175.

187 Koblik, pp. 45-78; Levine, pp. 60-73, 92-93; Kvist, p. 200.

188 Kirchhoff, p. 4.

189 Kvist, p. 210.

190 See, e.g., Levine, pp. 60-68, 93 ; Koblik, pp. 46-47, 53-56; Kvist, p. 202.

191 Levine, p. 105. In taking this step, the Swedish government may have been influenced by the Swiss. In September 1938, Germany and Switzerland signed a treaty under which Germany undertook to mark all passports of Jews with a sign identifying the bearers as Jews. Hilberg, pp. 54-55.

192 Levine, pp. 62-63.

193 Bertelsen, pp. 218-19.

194 Valentin, pp. 233-34.

195 Kirchhoff, p. 4.

196 Kirchhoff, p. 4.

197 Levine, p. 68; Undset, pp. 44-52.

198 Nordlund, p. 178.

199 Nordlund, p. 189.

200 Nordlund, p. 178-84.

201 Kvist, p. 201.

202 Kirchhoff, p. 5.

203 Kirchhoff, pp. 7-8.

204 Levine, p. 66.

205 Nordlund, p. 180; Kirchhoff, pp. 24-25.

206 In 1946, a U.S. dollar equalled 3.87 kroner; and the Consumer Price Index increased approximately ten-fold during this period. Using these figures, Max's monthly salary would equal $1,335 in 2003 dollars. However, this figure cannot possibly reflect Max and Nora's actual standard of living.

207 Wright, p. 10.

208 Wright, p. 10.

209 Petrow, p. 74.

210 A fifth column is "a clandestine subversive organization working within a country to further an invading army's political aims." The term was first used during the Spanish Civil War when Franco's rebels claimed they had four columns besieging Madrid and a fifth column within the city. *American Heritage Dictionary of the English Language* (3d ed. 1992).

211 Undset, p. 34.

212 Koblik, pp. 56, 61.

213 Undset, pp. 53-55.

214 Undset, pp. 98, 104.

215 Undset, p. 123.

216 Undset, pp. 143-44.

217 Undset, p. 166.

218 Flender, p. 7.

219 Yahil, p. 32.

220 Speech by Bo Lidegaard of the Danish Foreign Service, Scandinavia House, New York, Oct. 3, 2003.

221 Straede, p. 8.

222 Kirchhoff, p. 12.

223 Kirchhoff, p. 12.

224 Kirchhoff, p. 13.

225 Kirchhoff, p. 13.

226 Yahil, p. 207.

227 Kirchhoff, p. 13.

228 Bertelsen, p. 68.

229 Yahil, p. 241.

230 Bertelsen, p. 111.

231 In a letter to a friend written two years later, Johanna said the journey across the sound cost 2,000 kroner, which she paid after the war when she received

money from Norway. It is possible that Harald paid 5,000 kroner for his mother's rescue but asked her for repayment of only 2,000.

232 Bertelsen, p. 61.

233 Kirchhoff, p. 33.

234 Yahil, p. xviii.

235 Goodman, p. 221.

236 Harvey & Reppien, p. 170; Yahil, pp. 41-61.

237 Goodman, p. 223.

238 Stræde, p. 17.

239 Harvey & Reppien, p. 26.

240 Goldberger, pp. 177-79; Yahil, pp. 37-41.

241 Kisch, p. 217.

242 Wullschlager, p. 33; B. Ostergaard, Indvandrernes danmarkhistorie, Kobenhaven 1983..

243 Harvey & Reppien, p. 36.

244 Harvey & Reppien, p. 220.

245 Buckser, p. 192.

246 Straede, p. 18.

247 Speech by Bo Lidegaard of the Danish Foreign Service, Scandinavia House, New York, Oct. 3, 2003.

248 Bertelsen, p. 229.

249 Kirchhhoff, pp. 5-7; Levine, p. 70.

250 Levine, pp. 234-35.

251 Kirchoff, p. 14.

252 Kirchhoff, p. 17; Levine, p. 235.

253 Kirchhoff, p. 20; Levine, pp. 236-37.

254 Kirchhoff, p. 25. Contrary to legend, the Swedish government's decision to accept the Danish Jews was not due to Niels Bohr, the great Danish nuclear physicist. Bohr, whose mother was Jewish, was warned in late September that he was in danger of being arrested in Copenhagen, and he fled to Sweden on September 30. He immediately continued to Stockholm, where he went to the Foreign Ministry for the purpose of persuading Sweden to accept the Jews. By that time, however, the Swedish government had already made its decision. Yahil, pp. 327-28.

255 Kirchhoff, p. 28.

256 Even in Germany, during the years 1941-44 Jews in mixed marriages were not subject to deportation. Hilberg, p. 52.

257 Bertelsen, p. 22.

258 Leni Yahil describes how a large number of Danish Jews were admitted to Copenhagen hospitals under false names and hidden there until they could escape to Sweden. Yahil , pp. 241-46.

259 For descriptions of these procedures, see Bertelsen, pp. 100-19; Flender, pp. 63-160; Yahil, pp. 237-61.

260 Letter dated Oct. 8, 1943 , from Nora to Grete, Gerda, and Jack Poser.

261 Grunnet & Demer, p. 203.

262 Grunnet & Demer, p. 208.

263 Mentze, photos 255-267.

264 Mentze, caption of photo 267.

265 This heroic conduct is consistent with the record of the Copenhagen hospitals, which provided refuge to many Jews during the October 1943 rescue. Yahil, pp.241-46.

266 Until he moved to England in 1921, he was called Hans Poser. He anglicized his first name to Jack. Hans is the diminutive of

the German name Johann; Jack is the diminutive of John, the English equivalent of Johann.

267 http://www.ocean-liners.com/ships/queenelizabeth.asp

268 *New York Daily Mirror*, Aug. 3, 1954, p. 5

269 Apparently, Johanna was not aware at the time that the travel passport that she received in March 1943 from the Danish consulate in Oslo did not entitle her to Danish citizenship, but was issued solely for the purpose of enabling her to leave Norway.

270 My cousin Robert Salomon commented to me that after our grandfather's generation no member of the family could sell anything. In contrast to the enterprising Marcus Salomon and his sons Siegmund and Simon, the family has produced lawyers, administrators, and artists, but few who have shown a capacity for business.

271 Rasmussen, p. 24.

272 Laquer, pp. 301-12.

273 Laquer, p. 451.

274 Bertelson, Preface.

275 Reisel/Bruland Report, p. iii.

276 Speech by Bo Lidegaard of the Danish Foreign Office, Scandinavia House, New York, Oct. 3, 2003.

277 Vilhjálmur Örn Vilhjálmmson and Bent Blüdnikow, "Rescue, expulsion and collaboration: Denmark's difficulties with her WW II past." To be published in *Jewish Political Studies Review* (Jerusalem).

278 Yahil, p. 363.

279 Mentze, photos 60-61.

280 Flender, p. 7.

281 Buckser, p. 199.

282 Bertelsen, p. 74.

283 Yahil, p. 362.

284 Buckser, p. 177.

285 Following Samson's footsteps, his nephew, Gustave Alexander, served as the Mexican vice-consul in Oslo in 1927.

286 Information supplied by Professor Ole Harck from Hamburg archives.

287 Norman, p. 7.

288 A record of Sct. Hans Hospital dated Feb. 2, 1953, states that Alfred had a paternal uncle who was mentally ill and a paternal aunt who was suicidal. The uncle referred to apparently was Leopold Salomon.

289 The account of Betty Salomon's burial is based primarily on Oskar Mendelsohn's book, *The History of the Jews in Norway Through 300 Years.* Email dated Aug. 23, 2002 from Ragnar Areklett to the author; Norman, p. 20. Additional information about this episode was provided by my Norwegian research assistant, Marta Gjernes.

BIBLIOGRAPHY

IN WRITING THIS BOOK, I have used a variety of sources, including records in the national, regional, and local archives in Denmark, Norway, and Sweden; records of the Jewish communities in these countries; about 150 letters written during and after World War II, most of them to my aunt, Gerda Weill, from Scandinavia, mostly by my grandmother but also by my uncles and aunts; information given to me by historians and persons who lived in Scandinavia during the war; and the books and articles listed below, which provide an historical context for the story of the Salomon family.

The information about the family during the nineteenth and early twentieth centuries (Chapters 1 and 2) comes largely from the following sources: Norway: Oslo City Archive, the Norwegian National Archives, the Norwegian State Archives, the Oslo University Library, the Norwegian National Library, records of the Jewish communities; Sweden: the National Archive, the Regional Archives of Stockholm and Gothenburg, the City Archive of Gothenburg, and Mosaic Assembly of Gothenburg; Denmark: the State Archives, records of the Jewish community.

The information about the efforts of the Danish Ministry of Foreign Affairs and its Consul-General in Oslo to gain the release of my grandmother, Johanna Salomon, and my cousin, Hans Salomon, from prison in Norway (Chapters 7 and 8) is derived almost entirely from the records of the Danish State Archives. These records include files on "The Jewish Question in Norway," on particular members of the Salomon family, and on the ministry and consular officials involved.

The information about the lives of my grandmother and my Uncles Max and Harald and their families during the war is derived almost entirely from contemporaneous letters. It is also based on conversations and correspondence with Max's daughter, Frøydis Peterson, and Harald's daughter, Lilian Kulbir.

Most of the information about my Aunt Gerda's life during and after the war came from conversations I had with Gerda's daughter, Dorrit Berg, in 2001 and from my own personal recollections.

Much of the information about my Uncle Alfred during and after the war comes from the records of St. Hans Hospital in Copenhagen. I have used these records sparingly, however, to avoid any undue invasion of privacy. The hospital records also provided me with important information about other family members.

The information about my mother's life and tragic death is derived from conversations with my sister, Liz Gribin, and my brother, Joseph Poser, as well as from my own personal recollections.

Books and Articles

Abrahamsen, Samuel, *Norway's Response to the Holocaust: A Historical Perspective*. New York: Holocaust Library, 1991.

Arendt, Hannah, *Eichmann in Jerusalem: A Report on the Banality of Evil*. New York: The Viking Press, 1963.

Bamberger, Ib Nathan, *The Viking Jews: A History of the Jews of Denmark*. New York: Soncino Press, 1983.

Barford, Jørgen H., *The Holocaust Failed in Denmark*. Copenhagen: Frihedsmuseets Venners Forlag, 1985.

Benkow, Jo, "History of the Jews in Norway," *Scandinavian Review*, vol. 90, No. 3 (2003).

Bertelsen, Aage, *October '43* (Milly Lindholm, tr.). Copenhagen: Dansk Center for Holocaust-og Folkedrabsstudier, undated.

Bjørnstad, Ketil, *The Story of Edvard Munch* (Torbjørn Støverud and Hal Sutcliffe, trs.). London: Arcadia Books, 2001.

Buckser, Andrew, *After the Rescue: Jewish Identity and Community in Contemporary Denmark*. New York: Palgrave Macmillan, 2003.

Dawidowicz, Lucy S., *The War Against the Jews 1933-1945*. New York: Holt, Rinehart and Winson, 1975.

Denham, H.M., *Inside the Nazi Ring: a naval attaché in Sweden, 1940-1945*. London: Murray, 1984.

Derry, T.K., *A History of Modern Norway 1814-1972*. London: Oxford, 1973.

Dinse, Ursula, *Das vergessene Erbe: Judische Baudenkmale in Schleswig-Holstein*. (The Forgotten Heritage: Jewish Monuments in Schleswig-Holstein.) Kiel, 1995.

Encyclopedia Britannica 11th ed., 29 vols.) (entries: Altona; Copenhagen; Denmark; Jews; etc.). New York: The Encyclopedia Britannica Company, 1911.

Flender, Harold, *Rescue in Denmark*. London, W.H. Allen, 1963.

Gallenga, Antonio Carlo Napoleone, *Invasion of Denmark in 1864* (1864).

Garff, Joakim, *Soren Kierkegaard: A Biography* (Kirmmse, Bruce H., tr.). Princeton and Oxford: Princeton University Press, 2005.

Gelfer-Jorgensen, Mirjam, ed., *Danish Jewish Art: Jews in Danish Art* (W. Glyn Jones, tr.). Copenhagen: Rhodos, 1999.

Gerber, Jane S., *The Jews of Spain: A History of the Sephardic Experience*. New York: The Free Press, 1992.

Goldberger, Leo, ed., *The Rescue of the Danish Jews: Moral Courage Under Stress*. New York: New York University Press, 1987.

Goodman, Myrna, "Foundations of Resistance in German-Occupied Denmark" in *Rohrlich, Ruby*, ed., Resisting the Holocaust. New York: Oxford, 1998, pp. 213-37.

Hamsun, Knut, *Hunger* (Bly, Robert, tr.). New York: Farrar, Straus and Giroux, 1967 (originally published in Norway as Sult, 1890).

Harck, Ole, *Jüdische Vergangenheit – Jüdische Zukunft*. Kiel: Schmidt & Klaunig, 1998.

Harvey, William & Reppien, Christian, *Denmark and the Danes: A Survey of Danish Life, Institutions and Culture*. London: Unwin, 1915.

Hellig, Jocelyn, *The Holocaust and*

Antisemitism: A Short History. Oxford, 2003.

Kirchhoff, Hans, " 'Doing All That Can Be Done' – The Swedish Foreign Ministry and the Persecution of Jews in Denmark in October 1943: A Study in Humanitarian Aid and Realpolitik." *Scandinavian Journal of History* 1999, No. 1, pp. 1-43.

Kisch, Conrad, *The Jewish Community in Denmark: History and Present Status.*

Kjeldbaek, Esben & Thorsen, Kjeld, eds., *The Museum of Danish Resistance 1940-1945* Catalogue (Binzer, John, & Mesquit Teresa, et al., trs.). Copenhagen: Frihedsmuseets Venners Forlags Fond, 1995.

Koblik, Steven, *The Stones Cry Out: Sweden's Response to the Persecution of the Jews 1933-1945.* New York: Holocaust Library, 1988.

Kühl, Jørgen, *The National Minorities in the Danish-German Border Region.* Aabenraa, Denmark: Danish Institute of Border Region Studies, 2003.

Kvist, Karin, "A Study of Antisemitic attitudes within Sweden's Wartime Utlanningsbyran." *Journal of Holocaust Education* [Great Britain] 2000 9(2-3) pp. 199-211.

Laquer, Walter, ed., *The Holocaust Encyclopedia.* New Haven: Yale University Press, 2001.

Lauring, Palle, *A History of The Kingdom of Denmark* (David Hohnen, tr.). Copenhagen: Høst & Søn, 1960.

Levine, Ellen, Darkness in Denmark, *The Danish Resistance and the Rescue of the Jews.* New York: Holiday House, 2000.

Levine, Paul A., *From Indifference to Activism: Swedish Diplomacy and the Holocaust; 1938-1944.* Stockholm:

Elanders Gotab, 1988. (Dissertation for the Degree of philosophy in history presented at Uppsala University 1996.)

Loeffler, Martha, *Boats in the Night: Knud Dyby's Involvement in the Rescue of the Danish Jews and the Danish Resistance.* Blair, Nebraska: Lur Publications, 1999.

Mendelsohn, Oskar, *Jødenes Historie i Norge* (The History of the Jews in Norway). Oslo, 1969.

Mendelsohn, Oskar, *The persecution of the Norwegian Jews in WW II.* Oslo: Norges Hjemmefrontmuseum, 1991.

Mentze, Ernst, *5 Years: The Occupation of Denmark in Pictures.* Malmö, Sweden: A.-B. Allhems Förlag, 1946.

Nordlund, Sven, " 'The War Is Over – Now You Can Go Home!' Jewish Refugees and the Swedish Labour Market in the Shadow of the Holocaust." *Journal of Holocaust Education* [Great Britain] 2000 9(2-3).

Norman, Victor, *A Life in Music: A Lifetime of Learning.* Salem, CT: The Bayberry Design Company, LLC, 1999.

Norske skotøyhistorie i 50 år (Norwegian Shoe Industry Through 50 Years), 1951.

Pais, Abraham, *Niels Bohr's Times, In Physics, Philosophy, and Polity.* New York: Clarendon Press Oxford, 1991.

Petrow, Richard, *The Bitter Years: The Invasion and Occupation of Denmark and Norway April 1940-May 1945.* London: Hodder and Stoughton, 1974.

Popperwell, Ronald G., *Nations of the Modern World: Norway.* New York: Praeger, 1972.

Pundik, Herbert, *In Denmark It Could Not Happen: The Flight of the Jews to Sweden in 1943.* Jerusalem: Gefen Publishing House, 1998.

Salamon, Harald, "The Brigade's Drivers," in Niels Grunnet and Bent Demer, eds., *The Danish Brigade.* Copenhagen: H. Hirschsprungs Forlag, 1945.

Simpson, Harold, *Rambles in Norway.* Boston: Dana Estes & Co., c.1912.

Skram, Amalie, *Constance Ring* (Judith Messick & Katherine Hanson, trs.). Evanston, Illinois: Northwestern University Press, 1988 (originally published 1885).

Skram, Amalie, *Lucie* (Judith Messick & Katherine Hanson, trs.). Norwich: Norvik Press, 2001 (originally published 1888).

Steefel, Lawrence D., *The Schleswig-Holstein Question.* Cambridge: Harvard University Press, 1932.

Storing, James A., *Norwegian Democracy.* Boston: Houghton Mifflin Company, 1963.

Straede, Therkel, "Why Denmark Stood Up for Its Jews: Altruism, Pragmatism, and Anti-semitism – 60 Years Later" (speech given at Scandinavia House, New York, NY, Sept. 2003)

Sundt, Einar, *Norges handel og industri* (Norwegian Commerce and Industry). Christiania, 1907.

Undset, Sigrid, *Return to the Future* (Henriette C. K. Naeseth, tr.). New York: Knopf, 1942.

Valentin, Hugo, "Rescue and Relief Activities on Behalf of Jewish Victims of Nazism in Scandinavia." *YIVO Annual of Jewish Social Science* 8

(1953), pp. 224-251.

Westegaard, Waldemar, *Denmark and Slesvig 1848-1864* (1946).

Westlie, Bjorn, "How Norwegians Robbed the Norwegian Jews," *Dagens Næringsliv* (May 27, 1995)

Wullschlager, Jackie, *Hans Christian Andersen: The Life of a Storyteller.* London: Allen Lane, Penguin Press, 2000.

Wright, Myrtle, *Norwegian diary, 1940-1945.* London: Friends Peace International Committee, 1974.

Yablonka, Hanna, *The State of Israel vs. Adolf Eichmann* (Ora Cummings and David Herman, trs.). New York: Schocken Books, 2004.

Yahil, Leni, *The Rescue of Danish Jewry: Test of a Democracy* (Morris Gradel, tr.). Philadelphia: Jewish Publication Society of America, 1969.